Java Quick and Easy

Java Quick and Easy

A First Course in
Computer Programming

Chris Payne

ISBN 978-971-96780-3-8
(Paperback edition)

Because of the nature of the Internet, any URL's defined may
have changed since publication.

Opinions expressed in this book are entirely those of the author.

The typeface of the main text is Lucida Sans Unicode
The program code is set in Courier bold 10 point

Published by

Lipa Publishing
Helen Street,
Base View Homes
Lipa City, Batangas 4217
The Philippines

http://lipapublishing.com
Email : lipapub@yahoo.com.ph

Java Quick and Easy

Contents

Introduction

Java Quick and Easy

Introduction

This book is based upon a course of lectures in computer programming delivered to fourth year students of computer engineering at the First Asia Institute of Technology and Humanities (FAITH) in Tanauan, Batangas, The Philippines, over the semester November 2013 to March 2014.

The language chosen for the course, was of course Java, which is now the obligatory first language of study for students learning to program after only a minimum of previous programming experience. That is because of the ease of use and versatility of this excellent language. Whatever career a student intends, if it involves any branch of computer or software engineering or if the student is going to work in administration or commercial data processing, a background in Java will be of great value. Java combines all the features of programming good practice such as the use of abstraction, modular design and self-documentation.

Some teachers, when called on to teach programming to first-time students, will begin by teaching it as a theoretical subject. By supplying a firm grounding in the underlying academic methodology before the student begins practical exercises, so the thinking goes, the student will more easily learn to write tidy, correct and efficient programs.

I do not agree. Beginner programmers are faced with a lot of new concepts and ideas and do not need to be confused by unnecessary theory. In my experience, students learn best by the practical approach - learning by doing.

It is, in fact, the only way anybody learns anything. One watches and learns from someone who already knows how to do it. Then one tries oneself and makes small changes under the teacher's control. The method has been called 'sitting next to Nelly' but it is, at bottom, the only way we ever acquire new skills. The most successful way of teaching computer programming, I have found, is to get the student working on real programs as quickly as possible. The student does not need to know the fine detail of exactly what they are doing or why they are doing it, just as long as they can build personal self-confidence by writing successful working from day one. Software engineering is a practical-, not a theoretical, subject, one best understood by solving harder and harder problems and learning from one's mistakes.

This course is simple and practical with lots of illustrative examples and follow-up exercises. It starts with the traditional 'Hello World!!' and moves quickly to more 'sexy' computer programming applications which the students enjoy, such as graphics, animation, and network/Internet programming. By the end of the course the students should be able to write a professional graphical user interface like the application 'Jerry's Auto Shop' in Appendix B.

I have omitted references to systems analysis and design. The reason for doing so is because a novice programmer in their first job will need to interpret program specifications and to follow the organizational standards. Most software departments, even if they use some well-known methodology, will adapt it to the own particular requirements, depending on the company's software environment. The trainee will come to absorb it as they acquire familiarity with it and/or they will be sent on a training course. They will certainly not be expected to write their own design specifications until they are well-advanced in their careers.

Today's preferred design technique for object oriented design is the Unified Modeling Language or UML. It is the latest in a long line of systems design techniques - flow charts, decision trees and tables, structured English, structure charts, formal specifications, lambda calculus and so on. All have enjoyed temporary popularity for 10-15 years until they were replaced by the next big idea. That is the sort of time young programmers will spend programming the designs of their superiors before they graduate to creating designs of their own. By the time today's student gets there, the 'must-use' software design methodology of today will certainly have moved on.

Java Quick and Easy

The platform used here is the ubiquitous Microsoft Windows PC as found in most of the world's university computer laboratories. I have assumed that the version of Windows available is Windows 7/8 although this is not critical – any recent version of Windows will accommodate Java. The Java Development Kit (JDK) which is conventiently provided free by Oracle Inc, works well on most common platforms including Linux, Solaris, and others, although I have not included any mention of these.

This book will be of interest not only to undergraduate students of programming but also to students in high schools. It is published in both hard-copy and eBook formats and I hope that teachers will find it useful as a class textbook. For that reason, purchasers of the hard-copy version can download useful supplementary materials including lecture notes in Microsoft Powerpoint format, sets of laboratory examples, complete listings of program examples from the text and some extra worked examples.

In writing this book, I acknowledge a great deal of help from many people, not least hundreds of students who have sat in my classes over the years and whose names are mostly and regrettably no longer available to me.

Names which I do have include that of Dr. Kate Pulling of the Community College of Southern Nevada who very kindly read the proof version and made a number of valuable comments which I have included with thanks to her.

To my wife Loydz Suaco Payne, a continuous supporter of my authorial efforts, I owe a deep debt of gratitude for her assistance with the checking and layout of the typescript.

Chris Payne
Lipa, Batangas,
The Philippines
June 2015

Java Quick and Easy

Chapter 1   Getting Started

The first thing to do is to download and install the JDK (Java Development Kit) from the ORACLE Website. You need to point your browser at

http://www.oracle.com/technetwork/java/javase/downloads/

which is the main menu page for selecting your download. If you don't want to type this long address, it is easy enough to navigate to it from the ORACLE home page. You will see there a large menu of all the versions of Java which ORACLE distributes for free and there are different Java versions for all the common operating systems. This book was wriiten using Microsoft™ Windows 7 and so we need to download one of the two Windows versions. The 32-bit version is called *jdk_8u20-windows-i586.exe* but I have assumed throughout that the student will have access to a 64 bit operating system. The examples in this book all use the version *jdk_8u20-windows-x64.exe* for 64-bit operating systems. The examples in this book work equally well on 32-bit and 64-bit systems.

The ORACLE nomenclature is a little unsystematic but the Java Development Kit includes the JRE or Java Runtime Environment and the initials SE, which sometimes show up, just means 'Standard Edition'. The number 20 is the upgrade number of the JDK – version 1.8 at the time of writing. Oracle tends to update the version frequently, so by the time this book appears, the upgrade number will certainly be higher. Each new upgrade is usually no more than a small modification to one or more of the supplementary packages and does not usually affect the core language libraries which we will be using. It is not necessary to upgrade regularly with every change in this number. The download usually can take up to 30 minutes, depending on your machine and the speed of your Internet link. What I do is just to upgrade to the latest version every few months or so.

1

Click to accept the licence agreement and then click on the download and the JDK will be installed on your computer after a few prompts.

If you accept the default path for installation of Java, which is the easiest way to do things, then the JDK will be installed in a subfolder '*Java*' in your *Program Files* folder. This is a subfolder off the C: main disk directory. The address where all the main development software is located is the subdirectory

C:\Program Files\Java\jdk1.8.0_20\bin

In Windows, you need to add a PATH environment variable to your system variables so that the operating system knows where to find this subdirectory. To do this in Windows 7, you need to go to 'Computer' on the Control Panel. In Window 8, Click on 'System and Security'. Then choose 'System' from the menu and click on 'Advanced ' (Fig 1.1) to get the System Properties dialog box.

Once you have the dialog box shown in Fig 1.1, click the button marked 'Environment Variables'. This will bring up the dialog box shown in Fig 1.2. Highlight PATH in the lower window and then Click on 'Edit'. You can then edit the PATH variable in the upper box, by adding the string

C:\Program Files\Java\jdk1.8.0_20\bin;

within the existing PATH string list. Each path is delimited by a semi-colon. The place where you insert the new path is immaterial.

You are now almost ready to start programming. It is a good idea to keep all your work together in one place, so you might want to create a folder on the desktop called, maybe, '*Java*'. You will be using the *Command Line* prompt for your first few programs and it normally opens up in some directory like *C:\Users\Owner>* .

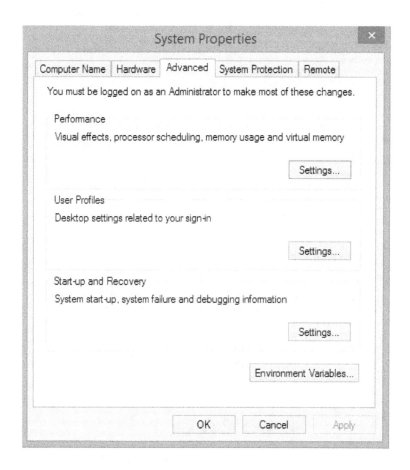

Fig 1.1 After Clicking 'System' in the Control Panel

It makes life easier if you write a small batch file which you run when you first call the *Command Line* window to change this directory to that of your Java main folder. Use an editor to create a file `java.bat` consisting of old-fashioned MSDOS instructions to change the current directory. My own setup has the *Desktop* in a subfolder of *C:|Users|Chris*, so my own *.bat* file consists of one command only

CD|Desktop|Java

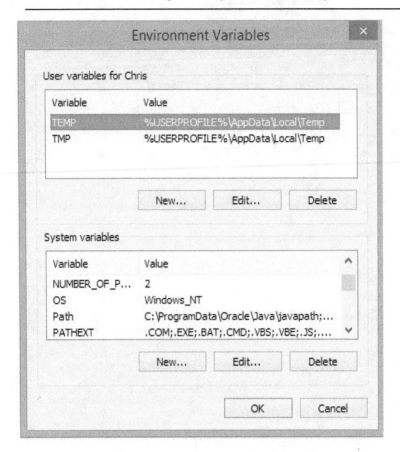

Fig 1.2   Dialog Box for Changing the Environment Variables

Then, if you type *'java'* when you first open the *Command Line* black screen, it will save you typing the path to your main *Java* directory every time you start work.

`HelloWorld.java` is the traditional first program you write when you start to learn a new language. It merely reports the simple message '*Hello World'* to your output device when you run the finished program.

Write the following program using a text editor like Notepad and save it as `HelloWorld.java` to your newly-created *Java* directory. The name of the class and the file must be identical. Remember that Java source files are case-sensitive – so be careful with the *Shift* key.

```java
/* My very first working program!!!*/
public class HelloWorld {
  public static void main(String[] args){
    System.out.println("Hello World!!!"); //main method
  }
}
```

Fig 1.3 Your First Program – `HelloWorld.java`

Then call the black screen *Command Line* window and enter

`javac HelloWorld.java`

at the prompt. This calls the Java compiler, **javac.exe.**

If you have errors in your code, they will be reported when the program fails to compile. Sometimes you get a whole long string of errors stemming from one small typo. If this happens to you, read the first error message carefully and it should give you the line number where you entered something incorrectly.

Correct the source code in your editor and try again. Do this repeatedly until the error messages stop. If your program compiles successfully, the screen just will return a new prompt. To run `HelloWorld`, type

`java HelloWorld`

and the program will return '*Hello World!!!*' on the next line. You are now a Java programmer!

What has happened is that the program **javac.exe** has compiled your source program to a file called `HelloWorld.class` which is now in your new directory. This file is composed of byte codes, a sort of intermediate programming language from which the program `HelloWorld` can be run. When you execute the line

`java HelloWorld`

the program **java.exe** computer executes the Java Virtual Machine, or JVM, which translates the byte code into the local Intel™ native code which the Windows machine uses. The program output is then generated by the JVM. Fig. 1.4 shows the command line sequence of instructions. Every different type of machine, PC, tablet, mainframe, etc. has its own version of the JVM but the byte code is the same for each. For this reason, Java is often described as 'write once, run anywhere' – unlike conventional programming language compilers which are specific to a particular type of computer.

```
C:\Users\Chris\Desktop\Java>javac HelloWorld.java

C:\Users\Chris\Desktop\Java>java   HelloWorld
Hello World!!!
```

Fig 1.4 The Command Line Sequence for Running
`HelloWorld.java`

Let us take a closer look at `HelloWorld.java`. The first thing to notice is that the program is actually called a 'class'. A class is a sort of template for the creation of 'objects', the programs which can actually do something. Within `HelloWorld.java` is a single 'method' called `main()`, the start-point of the program which must always be present once only whatever the program size.

Not all classes have a `main()` method, only those which are to be executed. Classes without `main()`, will be components within bigger programs. The word `public` indicates that the method or class is visible to and can be used by other classes.

The class is the model for the creation of objects by a process called 'instantiation'. When we compile our Java class from a `.java` to a `.class` file, we are instantiating an 'object'. A single `.java` file can generate any number of identical objects.

Sometimes we need to add another method, the 'constructor' to the source code to define the initial state of the instantiated object. We don't need a separate constructor in `HelloWorld.java` because the program is so simple.

The word `static` is used to specify that the method `main()` has a single fixed location in memory. This is important if the computer's operating system is to know where the entry point of the executable program is to be found.

A method is `void` if it does not return a value, something we will come back to later. The term `(String[] args)` allows us to add string arguments to the executable command line. (See Chapter 3),

`System` is specific to the machine you are using. `It` is essential when we are first starting to use Java and for on-going program development. The qualifiers of `System` - `'.out.println(..)'` - indicate output to a standard device, the screen, buffered a line at a time with a carriage return/line feed (CRLF) - ENTER as the terminating character for each line. There is also `System.out.print(..)` which does not move the screen cursor to a new line after execution. These two instructions are probably the most commonly used of all Java commands. The contents of the parentheses are of type `String i.e.` alphanumeric characters within quotes. We will see in Chapter 2 that this instruction is very versatile because it converts numeric data e.g. decimals, to a `String` automatically.

Anything contained between the symbols /* and */ is for information only. It is a comment ignored by the compiler. Any text appearing on the same line after '//' is also ignored.

In the `HelloWorld` example, the `main()` method forms a block defined between two '{..}' characters. For every '{', there is a corresponding '}' which lines up above the first letter of the next block definition, in this case, the letter 'p' of 'public'. Two characters of indentation are carried with every new block. The second 'public' is indented two characters from the line above it while the 's' of 'System' lies two characters further in. If you stick to that layout, your code will look clean and readable and it will be easier to debug.

Java Quick and Easy

The exercises for this chapter are practice in editing, compiling and running modifications of `HelloWorld.java`. Be sure to remember that the file name and class name must be the same.

Chapter 1   Exercises

Write, compile and run Java programs to do the following. Call your files/classes `Chapter1Q1.java`, `Chapter1Q2.java` etc.

1. Output 'Hello World' twenty times on twenty separate lines.

2. Write your full name on two or more separate lines.

3. Modify the program in Question 2 to separate each `String` by a blank line using `System.out.println();`

4. Write your name on a single line with two spaces between each part, using three separate `String` statements.

5. Draw a square of asterisks ten wide and ten deep.

6. Write your initials on the screen using capital letters to outline each initial e.g.

```
CCCCCCC  PPPPPP
C        P     P
C        P     P
C        PPPPPP
C        P
C        P
CCCCCCC  P
```

Chapter 2   The Basics of Java Programming

Java Data Types

The syntax and the structure of Java are based on those of the language C++ but Java is simpler and the core structure is easier to use. This is because although C++ is an object-oriented programming language, it was not designed as such. It is an amalgam of the older, systems programming language C, which was developed along with the *UNIX* operating system in the early 1970's and object-oriented extensions which turned C into C++ in the mid 1980's. The designers of Java set out to create a pure object-oriented language but, entirely sensibly, they saw no reason not to use many of the language structures of C and C++ which were already familiar to working programmers.

A Java class will be made up of variables which are data values used in the program, and methods, parts of the class which do individual tasks.

The variables can be simple primitive values which are single-valued items – numeric, character or Boolean types. There are eight different primitive variable types. (See Fig. 2.1). The variables may also be data structures like Strings, arrays, files, data streams or other objects. Methods are the small subprograms of a source .java class which manipulate the data and make it possible to solve large programming problems. The best way to solve a big problem is to split it up into smaller problems. The methods inside a class definition are the solutions to these smaller problems. The smaller the methods, the easier they are made correct and reliable.

Before use, all variables must be declared e.g.

```
int thisInteger;
```

Type	Size (bytes)	Range
boolean	1	TRUE or FALSE
byte	1	0 - 255
char	2	0 - 65535 UNICODE characters
short	2	-32768 to 32767
int	4	-2^{31} to $+2^{31}-1$ or -2,147,483,648 to +2,147,483,647
long	8	-2^{63} to $+2^{63}-1$ or - 9,223,372,036,854,775,808 to + 9,223,372,036,854,775,807
float	4	approx $\pm10^{\pm38}$ with precision of 7/8 DP
double	8	approx $\pm10^{\pm308}$ with precision of 15/16 DP

Fig 2.1 The 'Primitive' Java Variable Data Types

After this declaration, it can be assigned a value.

```
thisInteger = 45678;
```

Alternatively, one can make the declaration and assignment into one statement :

```
int thisInteger = 45678;
```

Note that every statement ends with a semi-colon.

The `String` type (Actually, `String` is a class, not a primitive variable, which is why it is written with a capital) can also define literal values between quotation characters e.g.

```
String s = "Hello Mom!";
```

or

```
String s =  "\"This is in quotes "\";
```

The second example shows how to include inverted commas inside a `String` using '\' to prefix special characters like '\n' – a new line.

By convention, datanames begin with a small letter and other words in the name definition should start with a capital. (This is the so-called 'camel' format.) Variable names must not be Java reserved words, they must not begin with a numeral and must only contain alphanumeric characters plus the hyphen or underscore. Spaces are not allowed and the whole name is case-sensitive. Constant values which do not vary for the duration of the program's execution can be declared using the word `final` before the type definition e.g.

```
final double PI = 3.14159;
```

Constant value names are, by convention, capitalized.

Java is what is called 'strongly typed'. This means that all instructions should consist of values in a single type only. However, this rule, if enforced strictly, would make the language unwieldy since there would need to be special methods for every instance of data conversion. With eight basic types, this would mean 56 different conversion rules. There are conversion methods in what are called 'wrapper' classes, as described in Chapter 3 but it makes common sense to allow for some basic type conversions and some 'mixed' expressions in the interests of simplicity. For example, if I wanted to find the average of a set of real numbers, I would need to divide the decimal value of the sum, a floating-point `double` value called `doubleSum` by the `int` value of the sample size, `integerSetSize`, I could use a simple instruction like

```
double average = doubleSum/integerSetSize;
```

There is also type promotion, as in the following example

```
byte a = 40, b = 60;
int c = a + b:
```

and, under certain circumstances, types can be 'cast' i.e. they can be converted to another type which is at least as long in byte length e.g.

```
byte b;
char c = (char) b;
```

The two types, byte and char, are distinct in Java. If b contains the value 65, then the char value of c will be 'A'. The '(..)' notation is important for 'casting' of one type of variable or object, to another where such a conversion is permitted e.g.

```
int anInteger = (int) aDouble;
```

Characters in Java are in UNICODE, the two–byte code which allows Java users to 'internationalize' text and other documents by allowing them to use all the world's different alphabets plus many of the symbols used in mathematics and currency *etc.* Most of the symbols in general use throughout the world have their own UNICODE values between 0 and 65535, including the symbols to represent Eastern ideogram–based languages like Chinese. The first byte of the first 256 UNICODE characters is '00000000' which makes them equivalent to the US–ASCII character set.

Java Control Structures

Java follows the conventions of structured programming for its control structures. Since the 1970's it has been normal to allow for only three basic structures – sequence, selection and iteration. Structured programming was developed then as a way of organizing computer programs into a more logical and systematic manner than had been the practice in earlier languages. The problem with the programming languages which were in common use prior to about 1970 had been the availability of the infamous goto statement which had been freely and dangerously used.

The languages C and Pascal, which appeared about that time, showed that the goto could be dispensed with. The problem with it had been its great range. This had not been a factor when programs had been small and thus easy to correct and service. But the increasing power of the third generation of computers (roughly from the 1960's to the 1980's) meant that program sizes were growing fast and program sequences could traverse thousands of lines via a single goto instruction. The result was programs which were becoming increasingly unreliable because they were getting too big and too difficult to maintain. The resulting logic 'rats nest' of too many goto's in a single program led to what was was described as 'spaghetti' code. Above a certain size, spaghetti code programs became too complex to be debugged thoroughly and sometimes their safety could amount to little more than wishful thinking.

Since that time, the goto statement has been outlawed and most modern applications programmers would never use it. It is now only found when programming in low-level machine codes as used, for example, for writng small embedded programs or 'firmware'. Most modern programming languages, including Java, do not even include goto in their instruction sets.

There are three basic selection instructions where the program logic may make a choice between two different logical sequences. The first is the if command, which may stand alone or with an else alternative. The basic form is

```
if (logical statement) {..}
```

The *(logical statement)* is a logical proposition and if it is true, then the code in the {..} curly brackets will be executed. If it is false, no action results. The variant of the basic form includes an else which is executed if *(logical statement)* is false.

```
if (logical statement) {..}
else
{..}
```

There can be `if` instructions inside both halves of this form. I recommend the student programmer to try to keep the nesting of `if`'s within `if`'s to the very minimum. Complex logic can often be simplified by splitting layers of dependent `if`'s into separate statements.

If there are multiple values of a single variable, a `switch` statement is preferred to the `if` command. This `switch` statement will allow the programmer to select from N different values of `someVariable`, which could take values e.g. `value1, value2... valueN` in the following example. Each `case` in a `switch` statement is an alternative depending on the value of the variable. If `valueX` (X=1..N) equals `someVariable` then its code will be executed,

After the statement sequence has been executed, `break` exits from the loop so that the program does not test subsequent values of the variable. The final line with `default` is optional and stands for 'none of the above'.

```
switch (someVariable){
  case (value1):
      /* statement sequence ending with */
      break;
      // multiple case and break statements
      . . . . . . . . . . . . . . . . . . .
  case (valueN):
      /* statement sequence ending with */
      break;
      default: // statement sequence (optional)
  }
```

Another important control structure is `try....catch` which is used to trap exceptions, or possible failures, usually, but not always, involving input/output. Its format is

```
try {  /*successful operation code*/
}
catch(Exception sE){
      /*exception handling code*/
}
```

Java Quick and Easy

The `try...catch` construct is used when something could go wrong and the program has to continue working instead of just crashing. These days software is used for all kinds of life-critical unmanned applications which must be foreseen and allowed for. The `(Exception sE)` condition could be any of many examples of the `Exception` class such as an attempt to divide by zero, file not found, wrong input format and many others. Every possible `Exception` can be handled by Java using this mechanism. A `try` clause may have several `catch` clauses to handle different types of exception.

There are three iteration controls:

```
while(logical statement is true) ( ...}
do {...} while (logical statement is true)
for(initialization,condition,iteration) {...}
```

with the following basic syntaxes for a simple output loop. All three of them give the same output.

```
int i = 0;                          // while loop
while (i < 10){
   System.out.println("Number = " + i);
   i++;
}
. . . . . . . . . . . . . . . . . . . . . . . . . . . . . . . . . . . . . .

int i = 0;                          // do-while loop
do{
   System.out.println("Number = " + i);
   i++;
}while (i < 10);
. . . . . . . . . . . . . . . . . . . . . . . . . . . . . . . . . . . . . .

for (int i = 0; i < 10; i++){       // for-loop
   System.out.println("Number = " + i);
}
```

There is also **break** which we can insert in any control structure as as we did in the `switch` statement above.

```
someLabel: while (someCondition){
           . . . . . . . . . . . . . . . .
           if (someCondition2){
                   break someLabel:
                   . . . . . . . . . . . .
           } // end if
           . . . . . . . . . . . .
           } // end while
```

This feature might be used, for example, when you have a long iteration statement and you are searching for some value. Once found, the loop can be exited to save time. The label name, 'someLabel', is programmer defined.

Arithmetic and Logical operators

The main arithmetic operators, for use in assignment or arithmetic statements are given below. Some operations e.g. bitwise operations, are not included here.

```
{+,  -,  *, /, %, ++,--}
{add,subtract,multiply,divide,modulo,plus 1,minus 1}
```

The equality and inequality operators take their usual forms.

```
{ ==, !=, >, <, >=, <= }  :
{equals, not equal, greater than, less than,
        greater than or equal, less than or equal}
```

There are three boolean logical operators for more complex logical conditions. They are

&& = 'AND' ; || = 'OR' ; ! is 'NOT'.

For example, if an 'if' condition, we might write

```
if (((a >= 4) && (b < 7)) !! (key != 'G')){...}
```

16

Java Quick and Easy

which stands for the multiple condition that 'both a is greater or equal to 4 and b is less than 7, or that key is not equal to 'G''.

Choice of two alternatives to a logical or arithmetic expression is provided by ? as in the following construction. If the denominator is zero, the ratio is set equal to zero. Otherwise, the ratio is calculated as normal. The two sides of the 0 ? 0 phrase stands for "zero ? not zero".

```
ratio = denom == 0 ? 0 : num/denom;
```

Java's Block Structure

The basic libraries supplied with the ORACLE Java SDK are collected into '**packages**' which must be import'ed before use. Third-party packages written by others may also be used, if one has the authorization. The standard packages contain all the basic class libraries one would ever need for everyday programming.

We write the source Java program and give it a name e.g. MyProgram.java. The compiled version of MyProgram.java is in a file called MyProgram.class. The basic structure of MyProgram.java is

```
import somePackage; // package imports
public class MyProgram {
  public MyProgram(){
  }   // the constructor method
    . . . . . . . . . . . . . . . . . . . . . . .
      // other methods of MyProgram
  public static void main(String[] args){
    MyProgram mP = new MyProgram();
  }
}
```

Fig 2.2 The Basic Java Class Structure

The MyProgram.java class could also be declared as private and thus unavailable to other classes and users. Default access is public.

After the class declaration comes a method which just carries the class name preceded by the word public. This is the constructor, – the method used by the main() method to instantiate the program object from its class definition. It can be omitted if it contains no code, as was the case of the class HelloWorld.java. However, it is needed, for example, when a program environment needs to be defined, such as a Window of a certain size, shape and color or when variables need to be initialized. (See Chapter 7) We can define other methods inside MyProgram.java should they be needed. These methods can be called by each other or by other programs.

The main() method runs the program. Its one line of code instantiates the MyProgram.class from its constructor.

Constructors are also needed to instantiate imported objects as in the following example. In it, we create a reusable class for calculating the area and circumference of a circle. We then use this class in a second class definition. The first class is called Circle and is saved as Circle.java. It has no main() method because it is not intended to be a program in its own right. Each of its two methods, area and circumference, is 'value returning' of type double i.e. they return answers once they have a value of the radius.

Methods which do not return a value are defined as 'void'

```
public class Circle{
  final double PI = 3.15159;
  public double circumference(double radius){
    return 2.0*radius*PI; // this method does a single job
  }
  public double area(double radius) {
    return PI*radius*radius;
  }
}
```

Fig 2.3 The Class Circle.java

The second program defines a new object c, of class Circle so that UseCircle.java now has access to the two methods of Circle.java. The methods of Circle.java are now available to UseCircle.java

18

using the 'dot' notation. The class definition `UseCircle.java` has a constructor which does nothing except define a value of the `radius`.

```java
public class UseCircle {
  double rad, ar, ci; // radius, area, circumference
  Circle c = new Circle();      //a new object Circle
  public UseCircle() {
    rad = 10.0;                  // set the radius at 10.0
  }
  public void run() {
    ar = c.area(rad);            // methods of Circle
    ci = c.circumference(rad);   // dot notation
    System.out.println("The area is " + ar);
    System.out.println("The circumference is " + ci);
  }
  public static void main(String[] args) {
    UseCircle uC = new UseCircle(); // dot notation
    uC.run();
  }
}
```

Fig 2.4 The Use of `Circle.java` *in another Class*

```
The area is 315.159
The circumference is 63.031800000000004
```

Fig 2.5 The Output of `UseCircle.java`

Note that the two double values, `ar` and `ci` are automatically converted to `String`'s by the `System.out.println(..)` commands.

Chapter 2   Exercises

1. List all the numbers from 1 to 100 in a square, 10 to a line. The tens and units should be aligned vertically.

2. Count and output all the odd numbers between 11 and 6473 inclusive separated by two spaces.
[Use a `for` loop – i.e. `for (int i = 11; i<=6473; i=i+2){..}`]

3. List all the capital letters of the alphabet together with their ASCII values.[ASCII capital letters take byte values of 65 to 90]

4. List the letters of the alphabet from 'A 'to 'Z'. If the letter is a vowel then output 'vowel' otherwise, output 'consonant'.

5. List all the numbers between 1 and 100. If the number is divisible by 3, write 'Fiz' on the same line. If the number is divisible by 5 write 'Buz', also on the same line.

6. Define three int values called 'day', 'month' and 'year'. Return the date in long format i.e. if day = 22, month = 4 and year = 13, then the program returns '22nd March 2013'.

7. Modify the programs Circle.java and UseCircle.java to work for calculating the area and perimeter of a rectangle and called Rectangle.java and UseRectangle.java.

8. Define a number between 1 and 50 and return its Roman numeral equivalent.

9. Create three Java classes. The first writes your name to the console, the second writes your address, the third uses these two classes to output your name and address.

10. Define three int values called 'day', 'month' and 'year' representing a date after 1st January 1900 which was a Monday. Output the day of the week on which your date fell.

Chapter 3 Reading Data from the Keyboard

Using `System.out.println(someString)` will allow us to output data from a Java program to the console black screen. It follows then that there must be a corresponding method for input from the keyboard. There is, but it is not quite as simple as its output equivalent.

This is because Java is not a language for the microcomputer only. Gone are the days when a computer would have only single output/input devices. In the 1970's the computer was a machine which converted punched card input into printed output. By the 1980's the microcomputer stood between the keyboard and a screen monitor. These days, the microprocessor is used in a whole range of disparate devices with a multitude of input and output formats. The input may be from a sensor in your car or your washing machine or from a satellite link downloading data as with a GPS system.

The output may be visual, or it may be graphic or audio or it may just change a setting on a device. Whatever it is, Java is probably involved in the software somewhere. ORACLE proudly announces that Java is run on over three billion devices world-wide. Only a fraction of those will be conventional keyboard and screen workstations processing data in character or numeric formats.

The original designers of Java were faced with a problem when it came to input/output of data to their programs. They could have written data handling routines for every conceivable combination of peripheral device but that would have been a Herculean task. Even in the early 1990's, when Java was being born, the use of computers in all sorts of unconventional ways was already becoming widespread. Besides, the originators of Java could not have predicted what kinds of new applications were still to be invented. The writing of different I/O classes for different machines would also compromise the spirit of the 'write once, run anywhere' Java philosophy.

The solution they came up with was to abstract out the physical input and output data by providing basic data libraries for 'streams' i.e. data flows which are not machine specific.

So Java provides all the basic classes in its I/O libraries to enable designers to create any file type they might need from the streams of basic byte's and char's. Here is an example. In this program you enter your name and it returns a greeting.

```java
import java.io.*;
public class InputFromKeyboard {
  String name;
  public static void main(String[] args){
    try{
      InputStreamReader reader = new
             InputStreamReader(System.in);
      BufferedReader keyboard
                       = new BufferedReader(reader);
      System.out.print("What is your name?");
      name = keyboard.readLine();
      System.out.println("Hello " name);
    }
    catch(IOExceptione){
      System.out.println(e);
      System.exit(1);
    }
  }
}
```

Fig. 3.1 Input from the Keyboard

The code in Fig. 3.1 is a short program illustrating the use of the InputStreamReader which is a class with methods for handling streams of character input. The instantiation requires an input source which is, in this case, a stream named System.in. representing the standard PC keyboard. The data is to be buffered, one line at a time, so we instantiate a BufferedReader input buffer, here called keyboard to simulate the keyboard input. The buffer terminates with the CRLF character. When the ENTER key is pressed, the whole buffered line is read to the String value, name, using the readLine() method of the class `BufferedReader` which has been `import`'ed from the `package` `java.io.*`, the package for stream and file I/O.

Buffering is the way most computers handle keyboard input. Even the fastest human is glacially slow compared with the speed of the computer processor. The processing of key strokes one at a time is wasteful of processor time. What the computer operating system does is to store keyboard input in a memory buffer until it gets the signal, the CRLF code, to process a whole line of input in one go. While the operating system is waiting for the user to complete the line of input, it can get on with many other things.

The program in Fig. 3.1 also uses the `try...catch` control to test for exceptions. This is so-called 'defensive programming' where everything that could go wrong is prepared for. One possible exception is that the input stream is not available. If that happens, the code under the `catch` instruction reports the failure status and exits the program cleanly without 'hanging up'.

When we write 'io.*' we are importing the whole package. Alternatively, we could just `import` only the classes we need instead of all the classes of the large pacakage `java.io`. If we did, our import statements would appear thus:

```
import java.io.InputStreamReader;
import java.io.BufferedReader;
```

Whichever form we use will make no difference to the size of the compiled .`class` file. All that happens if you use the short form is that the compiler takes a little longer (microseconds only) as it discards the `import`'ed methods it does not need.

Input and Output of Numbers as Strings– the 'Wrapper' classes

Now that we know how to input *Command Line* data, we can use it to do something. The next example uses the data from the input stream to input a number as a character stream from the keyboard, to double the number and to output the answer. Here the `try...catch` control is important. If we are only going to import a whole number of type `int`, then the calculation will not work if the input stream has any character which is not a digit in the range 0..9. If the input were a valid integer, it would be input in the form of a `String`, so before we can double it, we must first convert the `String` representation of the number to a numeric `int`.

```java
import java.lang.*;
import java.io.*;
public class ManipulatingNumbers {
  public static void main(String[] args) {
    String sNumber,outString;
    int twiceNumber;
    try{
      InputStreamReader reader
                 = new InputStreamReader(System.in);
      BufferedReader keyboard
                 = new BufferedReader(reader);
      System.out.print("Enter a number:  );
      sNumber = keyboard.readLine();
      twiceNumber = 2*Integer.parseInt(sNumber);
      outString = Integer.toString(twiceNumber);
      System.out.println();
      System.out.println
              ("The number doubled is : " + outString);
    }
    catch(IOException e) {
      System.exit(1);
    }
  }
}
```

Fig 3.2 Entering an Integer and Outputting Twice its Value.

```
Enter a number:   43

The number doubled is : 86
```

Fig 3.3 Output of `ManipulatingNumbers.java`

The line

```
twiceNumber = 2*Integer.parseInt(sNumber);
```

shows the use of a conversion by a 'wrapper' class method. The keyboard input `sNumber` is a `String` which must be converted to its `int` equivalent by the method `parseInt`, a method of the wrapper class `Integer`. To convert an `int` back to a `String` as in the line

```
outString = Integer.toString(twiceNumber);
```

we could use the `Integer` method `toString`. Strictly speaking, this is not really needed here since the `System.out.println()` method automatically converts numbers in its arguments to `String`'s.

Each primitive type has its own wrapper class for conversion to other types or to `String`. They are

```
Byte Character Float Double Short Integer Long Boolean
```

We can now develop the program `UseCircle.java` (Fig. 2.4) to allow us to enter a `radius` variable instead of declaring it inside the source code. We have made some other modifications in converting `UseCircle.java` to this new version, `UseCircle2.java`, in Fig 3.4.

Main Methods of the Wrapper Classes		
The Numeric Types	Character	Boolean
byte byteValue()	static boolean isDefined(char c)	boolean booleanValue()
static *thistype* decode(String s)	static boolean isDigit(char c)	boolean equals(Object
int compareTo(this type)	static boolean isLetter(char c)	int hashCode()
int compareTo(object)	static boolean isLetterOrDigit(char c)	String toString()
double doubleValue()	static boolean isLowerCase(char c)	
boolean equals(Object)	static boolean isSpaceChar(char c)	
float floatValue()	static boolean isTitlecase(char c)	
int hashCode()	static boolean isUpperCase(char c)	
int intValue()	static boolean iswhiteSpace(char c)	
long longValue()	static char toLowerCase(char c)	
short shortValue()	static char toTitlecase(char c()	
String toString()	static char toUpperCase(char c)	
static *thistype* valueOf(String s)		
static parseByte(String s)		

The explicit constructor method has been discarded since it contained no working code. All the useful part of the program is now contained within the `main()` method, which means that the global variables can also be defined inside `main()`. Variables used by `main()` but declared outside `main()` must be declared as `static`, since `main()` is itself `static` and `static` methods can only use `static` variables.

We must convert the `String` keyboard input `sRadius`, to a `double` using `Double.parseDouble(sRadius)` from the wrapper class `Double`.

```java
import java.lang.*;
import java.io.*;
public class UseCircle2 {
  public static void main(String[] args) {
    double radius, area, circumference;
    Circle c = new Circle();
    String sRadius;
    try {
      InputStreamReader reader
              = new InputStreamReader(System.in);
      BufferedReader keyboard
              = new BufferedReader(reader);
      System.out.println();
      System.out.print("  Enter a radius:   ");
      sRadius = keyboard.readLine();
      radius = Double.parseDouble(sRadius);
      if (radius >= 0.0){
        area = c.area(radius);
        circumference = c.circumference(radius);
        System.out.println ("  The area is " + area +
            " The circumference is " + circumference);
      } // if
    }
    catch(IOException iE){
      System.exit(1);
    } // try-catch
  }  // main
}  // end class
```

Fig 3.4 UseCircle2.java

The program in Fig 3.4, imports the two methods from the class `Circle`. In the line

```
area = c.area(radius).
```

the name `area` is used twice, once by the host program where it is a variable of type `double` and `class Circle` where it is a value-returning method. There is no confusion here as long as the 'c.' qualifier is present. Some programmers like to use the word 'this' to distinguish between the two :

```
this.area = c.area
```

```
Enter a radius:   4.5
The area is 63.8196975 The circumference is 28.36431
```

Fig 3.5 The Output of `UseCircle2.java`

Number Formatting

The answers to our simple calculations in Fig 3.5 are not very tidy. The output of double values is unformatted, so the output appears as the full width of a double value – which is 15 or 16 decimal places. Fortunately, Java has a utility class `NumberFormat` in the package `java.text`

> ### Methods of NumberFormat
> ### from java.text.*
>
> format(float or double)
> getNumberInstance();
> getCurrencyInstance();
> setMinumumFractionDigits(int);
> setMaximumFractionDigits(int);

whose use is shown in the program `NumberFormatting.java` in Fig 3.6 which outputs numbers to two decimal places.

```
import java.text.*;
public class NumberFormatting {
  public static void main(String[] args)
    double d1 = 1.23456;
    NumberFormat form2D= NumberFormat.getNumberInstance();
    form2D.setMaximumFractionDigits(2);
    form2D.setMinimumFractionDigits(2);
    System.out.println(form2D.format(d1));
  }
}
```

Fig 3.6 Formatting Decimal Numbers

Input of Data via Command Line Arguments

Another way of entering data into a Java program is to use the
arguments of the *Command Line*. The form of `args` in the `main()`
declaration is an array or sequence of `string`'s following the execute
command and delimited by spaces on the command line. The program
prints them a line at a time. The `int` value `args.length` defines the
number of elements of array `args`.

```
import java.lang.*;
public class StringArgs {
  public static void main(String[] args) {
    System.out.println();
    for (int i = 0; i < args.length; i++){
      System.out.println("  " + args[i]);
    }
  }
}
```

Fig 3.7 Entering Data as Command Line Arguments

```
C:\Users\Chris\Desktop>java StringArgs A AB ABC ABCD ABCDE

  A
  AB
  ABC
  ABCD
  ABCDE
```

Fig 3.8 Output of `StringArgs.java`

Using the String Class

The String class is a large class with numerous useful methods to handle strings of UNICODE characters. The String class is final, which means that it may not be changed or extended to subclasses. Once a String is created, its component characters may not be changed. This is not a serious restriction because, as we have seen in the above example using System.out.println(..), A String can be simply concatenated using the '+' symbol between String's, numeric variables or char's. The different types will be automatically converted.

The next program shows the use of some of the methods of the String class. It reads in a long string of variable length and counts the number of characters making up the string; it extracts a substring and then returns a new string made up of the 1st, 3rd, 5th etc characters of the original string. Finally it lists the ASCII values of the last six characters of the string.

```java
import java.lang.*;
import java.io.*;
public class StringMethods {
  public static void main(String[] args) {
    String inString, outString = "";
    int stringLength;
    InputStreamReader reader = new
       InputStreamReader(System.in);
    BufferedReader keyboard = new
       BufferedReader(reader);
    try{
      System.out.println();
      System.out.println("  Enter a long string,"
              + "more than 24 characters long...");
      inString = keyboard.readLine();
      stringLength = inString.length();
      System.out.println("  The string"s length =  " +
                    stringLength);
      System.out.println("  Extract a substring "
        + " of characters 12 to 24 ...");
      outString = outString +inString.substring(12,24);
      System.out.println(outString);
```

```
      outString = "";
      System.out.println("  The odd numbered characters" +
                    " in the string are : - ");
      for (int i = 0; i < stringLength; i = i + 2){
        outString = outString + inString.charAt(i);
      }
      System.out.println(outString);
      System.out.println("  The ASCII values of the " +
                  "last six characters in the string...");
      for (int i = stringLength-6; i < stringLength; i++){
        System.out.print((byte)inString.charAt(i) + "   ");
      }
    }
    catch(IOException iE){}
  }
}
```

Fig 3.9 String Handling with `StringMethods.java`

```
 Enter a long string,more than 24 characters long...
AbCD5hFRtIo<'"'<vredGkeWHYTM:0*@UhTGIjp%6#$
 The string?s length =   42
 Extract a substring  of characters 12 to 24 ...
""'<vredGkeWH
 The odd numbered characters in the string are : -
AC5Fto"<rdkWYM0@hGjz#
 The ASCII values of the last six characters in the string...
106  112  37  54  35  36
```

Fig 3.10 Output of `StringMethods.java`

`String`'s are defined by double quotes, unlike the `char` type which has single quotes but both can be concatenated together (and other types, as well) to create new `String`'s.

As can be seen from the program in Fig 3.9, the `String` class provides a complete set of methods for `String` manipulation. `String`'s can be deconstructed character by character where character position is numbered from 0 to (`stringLength-1`). The `String` class need not be explicitly instantiated in your program.

Main Methods of the *String* Class

```
int length()
int indexOf(char c);                                    first appearance of the character
int lastIndexOf(char c);                                last appearance of the character
String subString(int startIndex,int endIndex);
String subString(int stratindex);
String toLowerCase();
String toUpperCase();
char charAt(int index)
String concat(String s );                               concatenates to existing string
String trim();                                          removes trailing and leading white space.
String replace(char original; char replacement);
```

Chapter 3 Exercises

Write Java programs to:

1. Input a floating point number representing the radius of a circle and output the circle's area and circumference to 2 decimal places.

2. Input a sequence of characters one at a time and concatenate them into a string which is output as each new character is read. Terminate the sequence with `*`.

3. Input a sequence of real numbers terminated by the character '*'. As each number is entered, the running total is output. Values are output to 2 decimal places.

4. Enter a sum of money greater than zero and < 10,000.00 units as an integer number and return the minimum number of 1000, 500, 200, 100, 50, 20 unit notes and 10, 5 and 1 unit coins to which it is equivalent.

5. Input five numbers and return their average.

6. Write a program to read in a double value with a decimal point and multiply it by powers of ten until the decimal point is in the last place. Use try...catch to test for number format. Then output the resulting value two characters at a time, separated by one space. So 12345.678 would be output as 12 34 56 78. The fraction 0.000345 is output as '34 5'.

7. Input a String s of any length and write its output in reverse order. So "Hello" is returned as "olleH".

8. Input a String s and return the total of the ASCII values of the characters making up the String.

9. Write a program to create a table of numbers between 0.0 and 9.9 in steps of 0.1 and their squared values. The numbers are listed side by side with two decimal places and decimal points lined up i.e.

```
0.00        0.00
0.10        0.01
......................
9.90        98.01
```

10. Write a program to input a String s of lower- and upper case letters. The letters may be mixed upper case or lower case. Then input either "UC" or "LC". If you input "UC" the program returns the original String with all the characters expressed in upper case: if LC", the string returned has all the uppercase characters replaced by their lower case equivalents.

Chapter 4 Arrays and the Math Class

Arrays are groups of variables of the same type identified by a group name. They are very popular with scientific and mathematical programmers because they allow for large volumes of data of similar format to be accessed in a very few instructions. Although the array variables can be of any type including objects, arrays are mostly used with Java primitive types. They can be thought of as a rectangular block of values. A one dimensional `int` array `integerArray`, of size 6 will contain six `int` values e.g.

2, –3, 13453, 56, 0, –199

Arrays must be instantiated before use by a `new` declaration, either

```
int integerArray[] = new int[6];
```

or

```
int[] integerArray = new int[6];
```

The program can access the individual values of the array by reference to `integerArray[index]` where `index` is a positive integer value between 0 and 5. Array values can be assigned like ordinary variables e.g.

```
integerArray[3] = 18;
```

which places the value 18 into the fourth element of the array, replacing 56.

Defining arrays with values can also be done in one simple step. For example, if you wanted to define an array of size 7 and class `String` containing the names of the days of the week, you could write

```
String[] daysOfWeek = {"Monday",  "Tuesday","Wednesday",
          "Thursday", "Friday", "Saturday","Sunday"};
```

which is faster than using a new declaration statement and seven different assignments.

The next program defines an array of 1000 randomly-generated double values in the range 0.0 to 9.99.. and outputs the average of these numbers. To generate the random values we use the random method from the Math class (see below), which generates random double values in the range 0.0 to 0.99..

```java
public class ArrayAverage1D {
  public static void main(String[] args) {
    double[] randomArray = new double[1000];
    double total = 0.0;
    double average;
    for (int i = 0; i < 1000; i++) {
      randomArray[i] = Math.random()*10.0;
    }
    for (int i = 0; i < 1000; i++){
      total = total + randomArray[i];
    }
    average = total/1000;
    System.out.println
      ("The average of the 1000 random numbers is "
                          + average);
  }
}
```

Fig 4.1 Program ArrayAverage1D.java

The answer is near to 5.0. The random values are not fixed and change every time the program is run.

Arrays may be of more than one dimension. There exist applications in some industries where array dimensions may run into the thousands, but they are not common. Mostly, two dimensions is the highest level we use. The array elements are defined by a row and a column and can be imagined as a grid.

The following example is of a two-dimensional array with three rows and four columns. Notice that the row index always precedes the column index – called 'row major'. The compiler processes a 2D array by columns inside rows, effectively converting it to one-dimension. Here we define 3 x 4 array of type `char` by means of the '{...}' notation.

```
char[][] letters =   {{ 'A' , 'B' , 'C' , 'D' },
                      { 'E' , 'F' , 'G' , 'H' },
                      { 'I' , 'J' , 'K' , 'L' }};
```

The array can be thought of as looking like this in memory.

`letters[row][col]=`

A	B	C	D
E	F	G	H
I	J	K	L

We can extract the characters one by one with a small piece of code:

```
for (int row = 0; row < 3; row++)
  for (int col = 0; col < 4; col++){
    outChar = letters[row][col];
  }
}
```

The data is actually stored in memory as a simple string 'ABCDEFGHIJKL'. The program will transfer the letters to `outChar` in a simple sequence, unlike what would happen if I were to interchange the two for loops when the letters would need to be processed out of sequence. Fortunately, the Java compiler is aware of this and will try to optimize your code for best performance. But it is best to be consistent – the rule is 'rows before columns'.

To illustrate the use of two-dimensional arrays, here is the two-dimensional version of the program in Fig 4.1. In this case, we set up a 100 x 100 array of random double values and average the whole 10,000 elements.

```
public class ArrayAverage2D {
  public static void main(String[] args) {
    double[][] randomArray = new double[100][100];
```

```
    double total = 0.0;
    double average;
    for (int row = 0; row < 100; row++) {
      for (int col = 0; col < 100; col++) {
        randomArray[row][col] = Math.random()*10.0;
      }
    }
    for (int row = 0; row < 100; row++) {
      for (int col = 0; col < 100; col++) {
        total = total + randomArray[row][col];
      }
    }
    average = total/10000;
    System.out.println(The average of the 100 x 100"+
            " random numbers is " + average);
  }
}
```

Fig 4.2 Program `ArrayAverage2D.java`

```
The average of the 100 x 100 random numbers is 4.987440006653185
```

Fig 4.3 Output of `ArrayAverage2D.java`

The `Math` class

Java provides for scientific and technical computing by the `Math` class. There is a full range of methods for trigonometric, logarithmic and rounding operations plus constants like `PI`(=3.14159...) and `E`(= 2.71823...). All the methods of `Math` are declared as `static` and they return `double` values.

The following example uses the `Math` class methods to determine the angles of a right angled triangle with horizontal length 250m and vertical height 78m., in degrees and radians. It also returns the length of the hypotenuse rounded to the nearest whole number.

```
public class MathMethods{
  static double sideA = 250.0;
  static double sideB = 78.0;
```

36

```
static double angleA,angleB;
static double hypotenuse;
static double angleADegrees;
static double angleBDegrees;

static double calculateHypotenuse(){
  return Math.sqrt(sideA*sideA + sideB*sideB);
}
static double calculateAngleA(){
  return Math.asin(sideA/hypotenuse);
}
static double calculateAngleB(){
  return (0.5*Math.PI - angleA);
}
public static void main(String[] args){
  hypotenuse = calculateHypotenuse();
  angleA = calculateAngleA();
  angleB = calculateAngleB();
  angleADegrees = Math.rint(Math.toDegrees(angleA));
  angleBDegrees = Math.rint(Math.toDegrees(angleB));
  System.out.println("Hypotenuse = " +
                      Math.rint(hypotenuse) + "m.");
  System.out.println("Angle A = " + angleA +
                      " radians" + " or " +
                      angleADegrees + " degrees");
  System.out.println("Angle B = " + angleB +
                      " radians" + " or " +
                      angleBDegrees + " degrees");
}
}
```

Fig 4.4 Program MathMethods.java

```
Hypotenuse = 262.0m.
Angle A = 1.2683670392540094 radians or 73.0 degrees
Angle B = 0.30242928754088716 radians or 17.0 degrees
```

Fig 4.5 Output of MathMethods.java

The next example creates a table of trigonometric values of angles from 0 to 90 degrees, correct to 4 decimal places. The conversion from degrees to radians has a cast from int to double.

```java
import java.text.*;
public class TrigTable{
  public static void main(String[] args){
    double sin,cos,tan,radians;
    NumberFormat form2D= NumberFormat.getNumberInstance();
    form2D.setMaximumFractionDigits(4);
    form2D.setMinimumFractionDigits(4);
    System.out.println("     degrees    radians    " +
                       "sine      cosine    tangent");
    System.out.println("     ------------------" +
                       "---------------------");
    System.out.print(" ");
    for (int i = 0; i < 91; i+=10){
      radians = Math.toRadians(i);
      sin = Math.sin(radians);
      cos = Math.cos(radians);
      tan = Math.tan(radians);
      System.out.print("      " + form2D.format(i) + "   " +
                       form2D.format(radians) + "   ");
      System.out.println(form2D.format(sin) + "   " +
          form2D.format(cos) + "   " form2D.format(tan));
    }
  }
}
```

Fig 4.6 Use of Math – `TrigTable.java`

degrees	radians	sine	cosine	tangent
0.0000	0.0000	0.0000	1.0000	0.0000
10.0000	0.1745	0.1736	0.9848	0.1763
20.0000	0.3491	0.3420	0.9397	0.3640
30.0000	0.5236	0.5000	0.8660	0.5774
40.0000	0.6981	0.6428	0.7660	0.8391
50.0000	0.8727	0.7660	0.6428	1.1918
60.0000	1.0472	0.8660	0.5000	1.7321
70.0000	1.2217	0.9397	0.3420	2.7475
80.0000	1.3963	0.9848	0.1736	5.6713
90.0000	1.5708	1.0000	0.0000	16,331,239,353,195,370.0000

Fig 4.7 Output of `TrigTable.java`

The Main Methods of the Math class. (All methods are static)

double sin(double arg)	int max(int x, int y)
double cos(double arg)	long max(long x, long y)
double tan(double arg)	float max(float x, float y)
double asin(double arg)	double max(double x, double y)
double acos(double arg)	int min(int x, int y)
double atan(double arg)	int abs(int arg)
double atan2(double x, double y)	long min(long x, long y)
double exp(double arg)	float min(float x, float y)
double log(double arg)	double min(double x, double y)
double pow(double x, double y)	double rint(double arg)
double sqrt(double arg)	int round(float arg)
double sin(double arg)	long round(double arg)
int abs(int arg)	double random()
long abs(long arg)	toRadians(double degrees)
float abs(float arg)	toDegrees(double radians)
double abs(double arg)	long min(long x, long y)
double ceil(double arg)	*Constant* PI = 3.1519...
double floor(double arg)	*Constant* E = 2.7182...

Chapter 4 Exercises

1. Define and output an array of 20 characters side by side with their **byte** value equivalents.

2. Write a program to read **int** values into an array of dimension 10 and print out the contents with four spaces between each number.

3. Write a program to set up two arrays, each of size 12. The first array has the names of the months and the second has the number of days in that month. List them on the screen side by side.

4. Write a program to input a **String** of up to 100 characters into a **char[]** array. Multiply the numeric values of the ASCII values of each character as it is entered. Then write the on-going product modulo 127 to another array of type **byte**.

Java Quick and Easy

5. Write a program to set up a 3 x 3 array of type `double`. Output the transpose of this array where the row and column indexes for each element are interchanged.

6. Write a program to input an array of type `char`. Input an integer smaller than the length of the array and output the array with its position shifted right by the number of positions of the input number. The program 'cycles' i.e. numbers shifted beyond the end of the array take up positions at the start.

7. Write a program to defeine a value of the radius of a sphere and use this value to calculate the volume and surface area of the sphere using the standard formulae

volume = $\frac{4}{3}$. π . (radius)^3 : surface area = $4\,\pi$. (radius)^2

8. Tabulate the function y = $e^{-x}\sin(x)$ for x = 0.0(0.05)1.0.

9. The infinite series for the exponential function exp(x) = 1 + x + $x^2/2!$ + $x^3/3!$+..+ $x^n/n!$+ . where n! = n(n−1)(n−2)...3.2.1 If x = 0.5, how many terms in the sequence will you need to calculate to get a value for $e^{0.5}$ which differs by less than 0.000001 from the value provided by the Math class `exp` function.

10. Write a program to find the roots of quadratic equations ax^2 + bx + c = 0 for input values of `double`' s, a,b,c using the standard formula

x = (−b $\pm$ $\sqrt{}$ (b^2 − 4ac))/2a.

Test for the different types of roots – equal, complex etc.

11. Develop the answer in Question 5 above to write a program to input a 3x3 matrix and to output its inverse if its determinant is not zero.

40

Chapter 5 Input and Output of Files of Bytes

The file is the most common way of storing data. Files provide a structure of labelled data storage which can be organized into collections in directories and subdirectories. Files can be composed of different types, depending on the application. For example, they can be made up of records as database files are or they may be filled with continuous audio or graphical data. There may be readable, writable, hidden, archived or system files and they may be secured by passwords. The operations on files include reading from, writing to, appending to, creating, deleting parts or the whole of the file, and copying. Java's file I/O system must support all of these operations.

A file includes a header which contains all the *metadata* about the file. This *metadata* may include its dates of creation and expiration, its size (usually in bytes), its accessibility to users, its coding scheme e.g. UNICODE or ASCII or pure bytes, its blocking structure and its ownership. What is contained in the file header depends on the file type and the way it is going to be used.

However, as far as Java is concerned, files are simply low-level streams of either byte's or char's whose use and structure is adaptable by the program designers. The methods of the class File are shown in the box.

Methods of File Class

```
String getName()
String getParent()
boolean exists()
String getPath())
boolean canWrite()
boolean canRead()
boolean isFile()
boolean isDirectory()
long lastModified()
int length()
boolean renameTo (File newName )
boolean delete ()
void deleteOnExit()
boolean isHidden()
boolean setLastModified(long millisec )
boolean setReadOnly()
String[] list
```

File has three constructors to allow the user to define files by name and directory location.

```
File(String directorypath)
File(String directorypath, String filename)
File(File dir,String filename)
```

Here is a simple application showing the use of File methods i.e. to return some of the metadata.

```
import java.io.File;
public class FileDemo {
  public static void main(String[] args){
    File f = new File("Demo.txt");
    System.out.println();
    System.out.println("  File name : " + f.getName());
    System.out.println("  Path : " + f.getPath());
    System.out.println("  Parent : " + f.getParent());
    System.out.println(f.exists()
        ? "  The file exists" :
          "  The file does not exist");
    System.out.println(f.canWrite()
        ? "  The file is writable" :
          "  The file is not writable");
    System.out.println(f.canRead()
        ? "  The file is readable" :
          "  The file is not readable");
    System.out.println(f.isDirectory()
        ? "  The file is a directory"  :
          "  The file is not a directory");
    System.out.println("  The file was last modified " +
                    f.lastModified());
    System.out.println("  The File size is : "
                    + f.length() + " bytes");
  }
}
```

Fig 5.1 FileDemo.java – *The Use of Basic File Methods*

Files are collected into 'directories' sometimes called 'folders'. In Windows the directory structure is a multiple tree structure. There is no structural difference between a file and a directory – the directory is a file whose records are the names and details of the files within it. Directories can contain other directories, called subdirectories.

```
File name : Demo.txt
Path : Demo.txt
Parent : null
The file exists
The file is writable
The file is readable
The file is not a directory
The file was last modified 1434078253442
The File size is : 1305 bytes
```

Fig 5.2 The Output of `FileDemo.java`

The following example lists the contents of a directory, indicating whether each entry is a file or another directory.

```
import java.io.File;
public class DirDemo {
  public static void main(String[] args){
    String dirName =
               "C:/Users/Chris/Desktop/Amazon/X-JQE/";
    File f = new File(dirName);
    System.out.println();
    if (f.isDirectory()) {
      System.out.println(" Directory of " + dirName);
      String s[] = f.list();
      for (int i = 0; i < s.length; i++) {
        File f1 = new File(dirName + '/' + s[i]);
        if (f1.isDirectory()) {
          System.out.println(" " + s[i] +
                              " is a directory");
        }
        else
        {
          System.out.println(" " + s[i] + " is a file");
        } // if-else
      } // for
    }
    else
```

```
    {
      System.out.println("   " + dirName +
                          "is not a directory");
    }  //if
    System.out.println();
  }     // main
}       // class
```

Fig 5.3 `DirDemo.java` – *Listing of Files in a Directory*

The output of `DirDemo.java` is shown in Fig. 5.4.

```
Directory of C:/Users/Chris/Desktop/Amazon/X-JQE/
JQE Archive and Graphics is a directory
JQE Images and Captions is a directory
JQECover.pdf is a file
JQEPaperback.docx is a file
JQEPaperback.pdf is a file
JQEShaperImages is a directory
~$EPaperback.docx is a file
```

Fig 5.4 Output of `DirDemo.java`

The Input and Output Streams

The Java package for input/output is called `java.io`. and it provides four superclasses for managing input and output streams, two each for the `byte` and `char` input streams. The classes for `byte` I/O are called `InputStream` and `OutputStream`. Their `char` equivalents are `Reader` and `Writer` which are described in Chapter 6.

All four of these classes are declared as abstract, which means that they cannot be instantiated themselves, they must be extended by subclasses which can be used in practical situations. The abstract superclass has methods which are inherited by their subclass, so that these methods do not need to be redefined.

All I/O is, in reality, `byte`-oriented and the original designers of Java did not include character streams when the language first appeared. But with the replacement of one-byte ASCII by two-byte

UNICODE for character representation and the fact that so many of the world's data files are character-based, it was found expedient to duplicate all file classes in both `byte` and `char` forms.

The two abstract classes `InputStream` and `OutputStream` have some 16 subclasses to handle all possible types of `byte` I/O. These include, `FileInputStream` and `FileOutputStream`, classes for file I/O, `PrintSteam` for sending bytes to a printer via the methods `print()` and `println()` plus two classes, `DataInputStream` and `DataOutputStream`, which have methods for I/O of Java primitive types in a `byte` stream.

The class `FileInputStream` has two alternative constructors for defining input files. `FileInputStream(String filePath)` allows the programmer to define a file by its location in the directory structure. `FileInputStream(File fileObject)` is used when the object, `fileObject` of class `File`, has already been defined. Both open an existing file for reading.

```java
import java.io.*;
public class FileInputDemo1 {
  public static void main(String[] args)
                              throws Exception{
    FileInputStream f = new
            FileInputStream("Demo1.txt");
    int n = f.available(); //file length in bytes
    System.out.println();
    System.out.println("Total available bytes = " + n);
    for (int i = 0; i < n; i++) {
      System.out.print((char) f.read());
    }                         // byte's are cast to char's
    System.out.println();
    f.close();
  }
}
```

Fig 5.5 `FileInputDemo1.java`

The phrase 'throws Exception' after the `main()` method is an alternative way of coping with exceptions if the program is not being written to respond to them formally by the `try..catch` control as we did in Chapter 3. Exceptions with file I/O can occur when the file is not found, or is access–protected or it may be corrupted in some way.

The file *'DemoText.txt'* is a file created using an editor like Notepad, so it appears as characters. But the `byte` stream reads each character in as two `byte`'s and the instruction `print()` converts these pairs of bytes back to characters. Because its name does not include a directory path, the program will throw an exception if the file *'DemoText.txt'* is not saved in the same directory as the program which uses it.

```
Total available bytes = 318
The file is the most common way of storing data. Files provide a structure
of labelled data storage which can be organized into collections in directories
and subdirectories. Files can be composed of different types, depending on
the application. For example, they can be made up of records as database files
```

Fig 5.6 Output of `FileInputDemo1.java`

Output of a stream of `byte`'s to a file is similar. Here we set up a `String` type for output and write it to a buffer array of type `byte`. Contents of this buffer are then transferred, one `byte` at a time, to the output file stream. In this example, the declaration

```
FileOutputStream f = new
                FileOutputStream("TextFileOutput1.txt");
```

creates the file *'TextFileOutput1.txt'* in the current directory and opens it for writing to.

```
import java.io.*;
public class FileOutputDemo1 {
  public static void main(String[] args)
                            throws Exception{
    FileOutputStream f =
        new FileOutputStream("TextFileOutput1.txt");
    String s = "Costly thy habit as" thy purse can buy."
      + "But not expressed in fancy. Rich, not gaudy,"
      + " for the apparel oft proclaims the man.";
```

```
    byte buf[] = s.getBytes();
    for (int i = 0; i < buf.length; i++) {
      f.write(buf[i]);
    }
    f.close();
  }
}
```

Fig 5.7 `FileOutputDemo1.java`

Sometimes it is useful to transfer a whole array of `byte` data via a single instruction. For example, in the last example, `FileOutoutDemo1.java`, we could have saved ourselves a `for` loop by writing instead just

`f.write(buf);`

The method of `String`, `getBytes()`, converts a `String` variable in characters to an array of `byte`'s called, in this case, `buf[]`.

Methods of Byte File I/O

FileInputStream

read()	reads a single byte
read(byte[] buffer)	reads to an array of bytes called buffer;
available()	returns number of bytes still available in the file from current pointer
void mark(int *numberBytes*)	marks the point in the file until numberBytes bytes
void reset()	resets the input pointer to the mark set by mark
skip(int *numberBytes*)	skips over the next numberBytes bytes
close();	

FileOutputStream

write (byte *b*)	writes a single byte
write(byte[] *buffer*)	writes an array of bytes buffer
close();	

We use a buffer to improve performance by choosing some size such as 2048, 4096 or 8192. Many hard drives, used for storing files, have an addressable sector size of 512 `byte`'s. Understanding the relation between the sector size and the data buffer is critical to an application's efficiency. For example, to take the extreme case, a buffer size equal to the sector size would be most efficient since every sector would be full of data. But the efficiency of the system, based on data transfer times, would drop by almost 50% if the buffer size were one byte larger than the sector size. The buffer would then need to be written to two sectors, the second of which would only contain one byte!

Since file transfer to external peripherals is many orders of magnitude slower than processor operations or those involving Random Access Memory (RAM), anything done to optimize transfer times by buffering will impact directly on the performance of the application.

A technique which is often used is called 'double buffering' when the buffer is filled and written to the external peripheral. While it is being written, a second buffer of data is prepared. Once the file transfer is complete, the second buffer over-writes the first. Buffer sizes can be defined when the stream is to be buffered by means of the following constructors.

```
BufferedInputStream(InputStream inStream)
BufferedInputStream(InputStream inStream,int bufSize);
BufferedOutputStream(OutputStream outStream)
BufferedOutputStream(OutputStream outStream, int bufSize);
```

Because Java is a general purpose computer language, it must be able to support all the file I/O standard operations as used, for example, in commercial data processing. With some adaptation, java can be made to work with all the usual file access methods – sequenced, indexed and random access. To achieve this last file access capability, the io.* package includes a RandomAccessFile class with two constructors:

```
RandomAccessFile(File f, String access) throws IOException
RandomAccessFile(String filename, String access)
                 throws IOException
```

The `String variable access` takes one of two values - "r" which is "read only" or "rw" which stands for "read-write enabled." Methods available to this `class` include

```
void seek(long newPosition) throws IOException
```

which allows you to set the `byte` position in the file. This position is calculated in random access file operations by some arithmetic calculation of a key generated from the access specifier. An example of how this works is when a large file of, say cars, is accessed via the plate registration number. The program converts the plate number to a disk position for fast access.

Storage of Primitive Data Values

The InputStream and OutputStream extend to two very useful subclasses for the I/O of primitive Java types. These are `DataInputStream` and `DataOutputStream`. Their methods take care of the relevant conversions from standard numeric IEEE formats where necessary.

Here is an example of their use. Instances of all the primitive types are written to a disk file. The file is closed, then re-opened and read back before its contents are output to the screen.

```
import java.io.*;
public class DataIODemo{
  boolean bo = true;
  byte by = 65;
  char c = 'h';
  double d = 0.12345;
  float f = 54321;
  int i = 66666;
  long l = 1234567890;
  short s = 1024;

  public void dataOut() throws IOException{
    FileOutputStream fOS = new
            FileOutputStream("DataStreamDemo.dat");
```

```
      DataOutputStream dOS = new DataOutputStream(fOS);
      dOS.writeBoolean(bo);
      dOS.writeByte(by);
      dOS.writeChar(c);
      dOS.writeDouble(d);
      dOS.writeFloat(f);
      dOS.writeInt(i);
      dOS.writeLong(l);
      dOS.writeShort(s);
      dOS.close();
  }

public void dataIn() throws IOException{
      boolean bo1;
      byte by1;
      char c1;
      double d1;
      float f1;
      int i1;
      long l1;
      short s1;
      FileInputStream fIS = new
              FileInputStream("DataStreamDemo.dat");
      DataInputStream dIS = new DataInputStream(fIS);
      bo1 = dIS.readBoolean();
      by1 = dIS.readByte();
      c1 = dIS.readChar();
      d1 = dIS.readDouble();
      f1 = dIS.readFloat();
      i1 = dIS.readInt();
      l1 = dIS.readLong();
      s1 = dIS.readShort();
      dIS.close();
      System.out.println(bo1);
      System.out.println(by1);
      System.out.println(c1);
      System.out.println(d1);
      System.out.println(f1);
      System.out.println(i1);
      System.out.println(l1);
      System.out.println(s1);
  }

public static void main(String[] args)
                throws IOException{
    DataIODemo dIO = new DataIODemo();
```

```
    dIO.dataOut();
    System.out.println("And the contents of file
                    DataStreamDemo.dat are ....");
    dIO.dataIn();
  }
}
```

Fig 5.8 A Program to show the Use of the `DataStream` *Classes*

```
And the contents of file DataStreamDemo.dat are ....
true
65
h
0.12345
54321.0
66666
1234567890
1024
```

Fig 5.9 The Output of `DataIODemo.java`

Chapter 5 Exercises

1. Create a file of characters using an editor and read it into an array as a `byte` stream. Then output the characters to the screen.

2. Write a short program to list the data files in your current directory and then, separately, list the subdirectories.

3. Input data from the keyboard. As each character is read in it is converted to its `byte` form and output to a file of `byte`'s. Print out the file using an editor.

4. Write a program to count the number of `byte`'s in a file and to output those `byte`'s as ASCII characters on the screen, ten to a line.

5. Write a program to read in a file of `byte`'s and output the values in reverse order.

Java Quick and Easy

6. Enter a `String s,` from the keyboard and convert the characters in s to elements of a `byte` array. Write this array to a file and then read back the file for output to the screen.

7. Write a program to input, with prompts, three blocks of data each consisting of a `double` value, an `int` value, a `short` value, a `long` value and a `float` value. Output each block of data one line at a time with two spaces between each value.

8. Write a program which will present you with screen prompts

Check Number :

Amount :

After each appearance of 'Check Number', enter an `int` value. After 'Amount', enter a `double` value. The `int` and `double` values are written to a file called '*payments.dat*'. The prompts continue on new lines until the 'Check Number' input is = –1

9. Create a random access file file of 256 `bytes` where the `bytes` have values in the range 0 – 255 in ascending order. Prompt for the input a number in the range 0 – 255 representing a `byte` position. Your program returns the `byte` value at the position entered

10. Create a file of 1000 `double` values in the range 0.0 – 99999.9.. using `Math.random()` and output these `double` values to a random access file. Input a number in the range 0–999. Your program returns the `double` value at the position of the number entered. Random access files operate on `byte`'s only so the `double` values must be read and written as arrays of type `byte`.

Chapter 6 Files of Characters and Objects

Although files of byte's are used in very many applications, numeric, graphic etc, a lot of files are made up of character streams. The data unit of a char is two byte's long and while conversion between byte and char streams is not a difficult task for a programmer, Java makes life easier by providing a duplicate set of input and output streams for char I/O.

As for byte I/O, the equivalent classes for characters descend from two abstract superclasses called, in this case, Reader and Writer. Practical reading and writing to files of char is achieved using the two classes FileReader and FileWriter which extend Reader and Writer respectively. Their constructors are

```
FileReader(String filePath)
FileReader(File fileObj)
```

and

```
FileWriter(String filePath)
FileWriter(File fileObj)
FileWriter(String filePath, boolean append)
```

The boolean variable append, if set to true, is used to add character output to the end of a file. As was the case for byte files, file input methods can all throw an IOException which must be declared using 'throws Exception' or caught with try...catch. Specifically, input file methods can throw a FileNotFoundException and output methods can throw a SecurityException e.g. when trying to write to a write-protected file.

The character versions of the two previous demonstration programs, Fig 5.1 and Fig 5.3 which were applied to byte's are shown below. They do exactly the same as the byte versions. The program FileReaderDemo1.java gives an output similar to that of Fig 5.6. In this example we have included a BufferedReader.

```
                    Methods of Reader and Writer
                                Reader
     abstract void close()
     void mark()
     void reset()
     long skip(long numberOfCharacters)
     int read()
     int read(char[] buffer )
     abstract int read(char[] buffer , int offset , int numberOfCharacters )
     boolean ready()

                                Writer
     abstract void close()
     abstract void flush()
     void write(int character )
     void write(char[] buffer )
     abstract void write(char[] buffer , int offset , int numberOfCharacters )
     void write(String s )
     void write (String s , int offset , int numberOfCharacters)
```

The method readLine() of BufferedReader allows us to read a data file as String's of char data, each delimited by CRLF. This String s is then output to the screen. When the end of the file is reached, the next String input will be null and the file reading process will terminate.

```java
import java.io.*;
public class FileReaderDemo1 {
  public static void main(String[] args) throws Exception{
    FileReader f = new FileReader("Demo.txt");
    BufferedReader br = new BufferedReader(f);
    String s;
    while((s = br.readLine()) != null){
      System.out.print(s);
    }
    f.close();
  }
}
```

Fig 6.1 FileReaderDemo1.java

The char equivalent to the program in Fig 5.7, `FileOutputDemo1.java` is shown below in Fig 6.2, here called `FileWriterDemo1.java`. The char file '*TextFileOutput2.txt*' is created and the `String` s is written to it, one char at a time. As in the example in the previous chapter shown in Fig 5.7, we could simplfy this program a little by the replacement of the `for` loop with the single command

```
f.write(cBuf);
```

which writes the whole character buffer with a single instruction.

The large number of classes for input–output operations is too extensive to include in a first course in Java. Many of them are used only rarely and in specialist applications. Other classes we might mention include the classes `PrintStream` and `PrintWriter` which are of interest because they include the methods `print()` and `println()` which we use for `System` *Command Line* output.

```
import java.io.*;
public class FileWriterDemo1 {
  public static void main(String[] args) throws Exception{
    FileWriter f = new FileWriter("TextFileOutput2.txt");
    String s = "We few, we happy few!";
    char[] cBuf = new char[s.length()];
    s.getChars(0,s.length(),cBuf,0);
    for (int i = 0; i < cBuf.length;i++) {
      f.write(cBuf[i]);
    }
    f.close();
  }
}
```

Fig 6.2 `FileWriterDemo1.java`

I/O of Objects

So far the I/O streams have been of primitive types as `byte`, `char`, `String` or primitives based on the `byte`. More complex items such as objects can also be saved or retrieved as `byte` streams. This requires a process called 'serialization', which allows programmers to write an object to a `byte` stream.

Classes which might be saved to a file must be declared as `Serializable`. `Serializable` is an interface with a single declaration and no methods or variables. All the subclasses derived from a `Serializable` class are also `Serializable`.

If a class is not so declared, then objects of that class cannot be saved and a `NotSerializableException` will be thrown if you try to. Saved objects are said to be 'serialized' and class objects recovered from storage are said to be "deserialized'.

```java
import java.io.*;
public class SerializableClass implements Serializable{
  String s = "This is a serializable example ...";
  int i,j,k;
  transient int t = 0;
  public SerializableClass(int a, int b){
    i = a;
    j = b;
    t = 2*a + b;
    k = i + j;
  }
  public String toString(){
    return s + " k = " + Integer.toString(k)
               + " t = " + Integer.toString(t);
  }
}
```

Fig 6.3 Defining a Serializable Class

The class constructor of this example redefines the four `int` global variables of the class. It also has a method which overrides the `toString()` method of `Object` which is the method used by `System` to convert objects and variables to `String`'s for output. When `SerializableClass.java` is instantiated, the method for conversion from `Object` to `String` is the version of `toString()` in `SerializableClass.java`.

```
import java.io.*;
public class Serialization {
  public static void main(String[] args){
    try {                              // serializing
      SerializableClass sC1 = new
                   SerializableClass(10,20);
      System.out.println();
      System.out.println(sC1);
      FileOutputStream fOS = new
                   FileOutputStream("outfileSc1.txt");
      ObjectOutputStream oOS = new
                   ObjectOutputStream(fOS);
      oOS.writeObject(sC1);
      oOS.flush();
      oOS.close();
    }
    catch(Exception e){
      System.out.println("   Writing exception " + e );
    }
    try {                              // deserializing
      SerializableClass sC2;
      FileInputStream fIS = new
                   FileInputStream("outfileSc1.txt");
      ObjectInputStream oIS = new  ObjectInputStream(fIS);
      sC2 = (SerializableClass) oIS.readObject();
      oIS.close();
      System.out.println();
      System.out.println(sC2);
    }
    catch(Exception e){
      System.out.println("   Reading exception " + e);
    }
  }
}
```

Fig 6.4 `Serialization.java`

The program, `Serialization.java` in Fig 6.4 first executes the program `SerializableClass` and produces the first line of output shown in Fig 6.5. The values of `k` and `t` are calculated to 30 and 40 respectively in its `toString()` method. The `SerializableClass` object sC1 is then saved to a `byte` file 'outfileSc1.txt'. This output file stream is then closed and re-opened for reading into an input `byte` stream `FileInputStream` which is cast to a object sC2.

After reading back the stored file, the value of the `int` variable `k` becomes equal to 30 which means that it has retained the value it had been changed to when it was calculated at startup which sets $i = 10$ and $j = 20$ to calculate $k = i + j = 30$. The other `int` variable, $t = 2 * i + j$ and $t = 40$ after the program is run. This is because t had been declared as `transient` which means that it is stored as its original value, not the value it had been changed to after it had been recalculated.

```
This is a serializable example ... k = 30   t = 40
This is a serializable example ... k = 30   t = 0
```

Fig 6.5 The Output of `Serialization.java`

Java and Data Processing

In data processing operations as found e.g. in finance or administration *etc.* it is usual to define a data structure of some record type. Records are used in many languages to store collections of different data items of various types. Java is quite a suitable language for conventional data processing even if it does not define an explicit record type. The serialization mechanism can be used instead.

The Java equivalent of a record is a `Serializable` class with variables only i.e. with no working methods. Classes for data record manipulation can then be written to perform the standard tasks of information systems processing - reading and writing to files, record deletion, file updating and addition of new records, reporting, indexing, sorting, random access procedures and so on.

The following example shows how to use a `Serializable class` to process data personnel data as one might want to do in a traditional administrative information system. The data record can be defined as follows.

```
public class DataRecord implements Serializable{
   String name;
   String address;
   String dateOfBirth;
   char sex;
   int recordKey;
}
```

Fig 6.6 A 'Record' Class File

The following program, Fig 6.7, is a Java program to write three objects of class DataRecord to a file.

```
import java.io.*;
public class WriteData{
   public static void main(String[] args){
     String nom,add,dOB,key,gender;
     try{
       InputStreamReader reader = new
                          InputStreamReader(System.in);
       BufferedReader keyboard  = new
                          BufferedReader(reader);
       FileOutputStream fOS = new
                          FileOutputStream("File66.dat");
       ObjectOutputStream oOS = new
                          ObjectOutputStream(fOS);
       for (int i = 0; i < 3; i++){
         System.out.print("Enter name : ");
         nom = keyboard.readLine();
         System.out.println();
         System.out.print("Enter address : ");
         add = keyboard.readLine();
         System.out.println();
         System.out.print("Enter date of birth : ");
         dOB = keyboard.readLine();
         System.out.println();
         System.out.print("Enter sex : ");
         gender = keyboard.readLine();
         System.out.println();
```

```java
      System.out.print("Enter record key : ");
      key = keyboard.readLine();
      System.out.println();
      DataRecord dR = new DataRecord();
      dR.name = nom;
      dR.address = add;
      dR.dateOfBirth = dOB;
      dR.sex = gender.charAt(0);
      dR.recordKey = Integer.parseInt(key);
      oOS.writeObject(dR);
      oOS.flush();
    }
    oOS.close();
  }
  catch(Exception e){
    System.out.println("File write error");
  }
}

// Read back the file to check the program

try{
  DataRecord  dr1 = new DataRecord();
  FileInputStream fIS = new
                   FileInputStream("File66.dat");
    ObjectInputStream oIS = new
                   ObjectInputStream(fIS);
    for (int i = 0; i < 3; i++){
      dr1 = (DataRecord) oIS.readObject();
      System.out.print(dr1.name + "   ");
      System.out.print(dr1.address + "   ");
      System.out.print(dr1.dateOfBirth + "   ");
      System.out.print(dr1.sex + "   ");
      System.out.print(dr1.recordKey + "   ");
      System.out.println();
    }
    oIS.close();
  }

  catch(Exception e){
    System.out.println("File read error");
  }
}
```

Fig 6.7 A `Serializable` *File for Data Storage*

```
Enter name : Albert
Enter address : 10 Downing Street London W1
Enter date of birth : 23/5/1955
Enter sex : M
Enter record key : 67
Enter name : Brian
Enter address : Buckingham Palace London SW1
Enter date of birth : 6/11/1948
Enter sex : M
Enter record key : 68
Enter name : Charlie
Enter address : Coronation Street Salford 4
Enter date of birth : 20/6/1977
Enter sex : M
Enter record key : 69
Albert   10 Downing Street London W1   23/5/1955  M  67
Brian    Buckingham Palace London SW1   6/11/1948  M  68
Charlie  Coronation Street Salford 4   20/6/1977  M  69
```

Fig 6.8 Output of `WriteData.java`

Chapter 6 Exercises

1. Create a file of `char`'s with an editor and read it into an array. Then output the characters to the screen. Write the array of characters to a file. Close the file, re-open it for reading and report its contents to the console screen.

2. Modify the program of Question 1 to format the output to lines which are forty characters wide.

3. Write a program using the file created in Question 1 above and prompt the user for an index of the position of a particular character. On entering the index, the program returns the character at that index position.

4. Write a program to read dates from a file each in the form of a six-character `String` DDMMYY. Output these values to the screen as a `String` in the format *Month+space+Ordinal Day+space+Full Year*. Thus the input '220314' will be written as 'March 22nd 2014'.

5. Write a program to output a `String` of indeterminate length to a `char` file. Two spaces are inserted after every fifth character. Insert a newline character, `'\n'`, after every second group of 5. Return the file as output to show the formatting of the data.

6. Write a program to define two character files. The first contains a random stream of letters 'A' to 'Z', of indeterminate length. The second is similar except that it contains a random stream of digits '0' to '9'. After defining the files, they should be merged into a third file with alternate letters and digits. If the files are of different lengths, the unmerged letters or digits should all be written to the new file. Read back the result to test your program.

7. Convert the `.java` file from Question 7 above to make it `Serializable`. Save the `.class` file and read it back. After reading, check that it still works.

8. Write a program to define a `Serializable` class called `CarRecord.java` which contains data including make, model, year of first registration, price. Then write a second program to create four records of type `CarRecord` and write them to a file called '*Cars.dat*'.

9. Write a program to define a `Serializable` class called `MyRecord` which contains `String name`, and an array called `payments` of type `double[10]`. Then write a second program to create two records of type `MyRecord` and write them to a file called '*MyPayments.dat*'.

Chapter 7   The Abstract Windows Toolkit (AWT)

Up until now we have had to rely on the *Command Line* for our program execution. Use of the System.in and System.out classes is essential to get started quickly with Java and the instruction System.out.println(..) will always be important, even for experienced Java programmers. Programmers often need to set points in their programs where they can observe intermediate values of their program variables and System.out.println(..) makes it quick and easy to do that.

But most modern program environments for the microcomputer make use of a Graphical User Interface or GUI. In a GUI, graphical objects share a desktop with standard Windows components such as labels, buttons, menus etc. In fact, the WIMPS (Windows-Icons-Menus-Pointers-Screens) environment is now standard in most forms of personal computing. The basic GUI is made up of 'objects' which include the Window container object itself, the menus, the graphics objects, the mouse pointer objects and so on.

In this chapter we will draw Graphics objects in a Frame. Frame is a subclass of Window which is itself a subclass of Container, the superclass of all those objects which are used to hold other objects. The hierarchy of Container objects descends from Component which includes all graphical Windows objects.

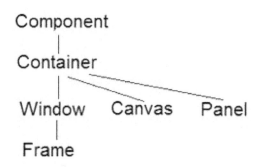

Fig 7.1 The Ancestry of Frame

`Window` has two other subclasses, `Canvas` and `Panel`. We will meet `Panel`'s again in Chapter 15 when we look at the `Swing` classes. Essentially a `Panel` object is a `Container` without title bar, menu bar or border. The `Panel` is also the superclass of `applet` (Chapter 13). A `Canvas` is a plain, drawing area whereon we can create `Graphics` objects. Graphics and Windows objects can also be drawn directly on to a `Frame`, which is the way we will do things in this chapter.

The Co-ordinate Frame for Graphics

Adding graphics objects to the `Frame` uses the fourth-quadrant Cartesian absolute co-ordinates. The (X,Y) co-ordinates are pixel measurements from the left and the top of the screen respectively.

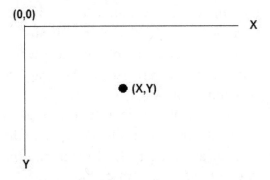

Fig 7.2 The Absolute Co-ordinate Drawing Frame

Objects defined on the `Frame` are positioned by their upper left hand corner and sized by dimensions width and height. The origin (0,0) is the top left hand corner of the containing `Frame`, usually the corner of the screen itself.

Using `Frame`

A `Frame` possesses all the `Window` characteristics including a border, a title, room for a `MenuBar` where menus can be attached, scroll bars,

Java Quick and Easy

the freedom to set foreground and background colors etc. `Frame`'s can be sized, located and made visible or invisible.

There are two constructors:

```
Frame();
Frame(String title);
```

Your own graphics programs extends `Frame` i.e. be a subclass of the `Frame` class. The appearance of your `Frame`, based on the methods in the box, will be defined in the class constructor. The classes `Frame` makes use of for setting its appearance include `Color`, `Font` and `LayoutManager`.

> **Methods of Frame**
>
> setTitle(String title);
> setSize(int width, int height);
> setSize(Dimension d);
> Dimension d = getDimension();
> setLocation(int xpos, int yPos);
> setForeground(Color.color);
> setbackground(Color.color);
> setLayout(LayoutManager IM);
> setVisible(boolean vsible);

The graphical display is drawn using the method `paint(Graphics graphicsObject)` which is executed when the Frame is instantiated.

Color

The `Color` class includes thirteen pre-defined constants of type `int` representing the standard colors:

```
black,   blue,   cyan,   darkGray,   gray,   lightGray,   green,
magenta, orange, pink, red, yellow, white,
```

More subtle colors can be created from the RGB palette.

```
Color (int red, int green, int blue);
Color (int rgbValue);
Color (float red, float green, float blue);
```

The separate `int` values in the first of these must each be between 0 and 255 but they can be combined into a single `int` for the second form. The argument `rgbValue` is a single integer made up from the bits in a 32-bit `int`. The `blue` value is defined by bits 0-7; `green` is bits 8-15 and `red` is bits 16-23. Bits 24-31 are all zero. The three `float` values take values between between 0.0 and 0.99, specifying the relative proportions of `red`, `green` and `blue` in the new `Color`.

Layout Managers

`Layout Managers` are discussed in Chapter 13. However, if we do not explicitly suppress it, the complier assumes that we are putting our `Graphics` objects on the screen using the default `FlowLayout`, where the objects on the screen are placed one after the other.

When we want to layout the screen using absolute screen co-ordinates, we must include the following instruction to suppress `FlowLayout`.

```
setLayout(null);
```

For the next couple of chapters we will be using absolute co-ordinates as defined in Fig. 7.2.

Font

`Font`'s define the appearance of text. The constructor for `Font` is

```
Font (String fontName, int fontStyle, int pointSize);
```

The range of available fonts varies between operating system environments but most host machines support standard fonts such as SansSerif, Times New Roman, Verdana, Courier, Arial and maybe some others. If you are working on a Microsoft PC, then the Windows environment allows you to use many of the extra non-standard fonts also. The `fontStyle` is optionally one of three `int` constants `PLAIN`, `BOLD` or `ITALIC`. These three can be combined, as in the following font declaration.

```
Font f = new Font("Times New Roman",
                      Font.BOLD|Font.ITALIC,28);
```

which defines a Times New Roman font with italic bold style and 28 point size. (There are 72 points to the inch.)

The `Font` constructor is also available to `Frame` . It is set in the `Frame` constructor by

```
void setFont(Font fontObject)
```

and it can be changed within the `paint(Graphics g)` method by the same command

```
g.setFont(Font fontObject);
```

so that multiple fonts can be used with `g.drawString()` in a graphical display as in the following example.

Graphics

`Graphics` objects in a `Frame` are under the control of the method

```
paint(Graphics g){}
```

`Graphics` is a class which supports all the main geometrical and text components necessary for producing graphical layouts. It must be `import`'ed from the package `java.awt`.

The `paint()` method is called when the constructor is executed and draws the `Frame` appearance at startup. Simple graphics programs have the following basic structure.

```
import java.awt.*;        // imports the awt and graphics
public class FirstGraphics extends Frame{
  public FirstGraphics(){//the constructor
    setSize(width,height)); //define Frame size
    setLayout(null);          //suppress layout control
    setBackground(Color.c1);//Frame background color
    setForeground(Color.c2);//color of graphics objects
    setTitle("The title of the Frame");
    setVisible(true);
  }
  public void paint(Graphics g){..}
  public static void main(String[] args){
    FirstGraphics fG = new FirstGraphics();
  }
}
```

Fig 7.3 The Basic Structure of a Simple Graphics Program

Here is a very simple first graphics program. What it does is self-explanatory.

```
import java.awt.*;
public class FirstGraphics extends Frame{
  Font f = new Font(Ärial",Font.BOLD,36);
  public FirstGraphics(){
    setSize(600,600);
    setLayout(null);
    setFont(f)
    setBackground(Color.yellow);
    setForeground(Color.black);
    setTitle("First Graphics");
    setVisible(true);
  }
  public void paint(Graphics g){
    g.drawString("Java Quick and Easy",100,100);
    g.setColor(Color.red);
    g.fillOval(300,300,100,100);
  }
  public static void main(String[] args){
    FirstGraphics fG = new FirstGraphics();
  }
}
```

Fig 7.4 `FirstGraphics.java`

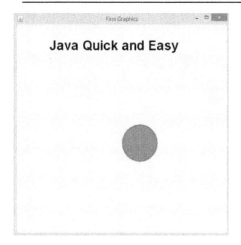

Fig 7.5 Output of
`FirstGraphics.java`

The `Graphics` class has methods for drawing standard geometric shapes – lines, ovals, rectangles, polygons and arcs. These objects are colored in the current color and closed figures may be drawn either in outline or filled.

`Graphics` also allows for text output via the `drawString()` method which permits you to output a text `String` at a point defined by the (x, y) values of its upper left corner. To format text defined by this `String` object, we can use the `Font` class.

```java
import java.awt.*;
public class SecondGraphics extends Frame{
   Font f1 = new Font("Verdana",Font.PLAIN,18);
   Font f2 = new Font("Times New Roman",Font.BOLD,24);
   Font f3 = new Font("Arial",Font.ITALIC,32);
   public SecondGraphics(){
     setSize(600,600);
     setLayout(null);
     setBackground(Color.white);
     setTitle("Second Graphics Program");
     setVisible(true);
   }
   public void paint(Graphics g){
     g.setColor(Color.blue);
     g.setFont(f1);
     g.drawString
       ("Font Verdana, plain, 18 point", 50,50);
```

```
        g.setColor(Color.red);
        g.setFont(f2);
        g.drawString
            ("Font Times New Roman bold 24 point", 50,100);
        g.setColor(Color.black);
        g.setFont(f3);
        g.drawString
            ("Font Arial italic 32 point", 50,150);
        g.setColor(Color.red);
        g.drawRect(50,250,50,50);
        g.setColor(Color.green);
        g.fillRect(150,250,50,50);
        g.setColor(Color.black);
        g.drawOval(50,350,50,50);
        g.setColor(Color.magenta);
        g.fillOval(150,350,50,50);
        g.setColor(Color.cyan);
        g.drawRect(50,450,50,50);
        g.setColor(Color.orange);
        g.fillRect(150,450,50,50);
    }
    public static void main(String[] args){
        SecondGraphics sG = new SecondGraphics();
    }
}
```

Fig 7.6 The Program `SecondGraphics.java`

Fig 7.7 The Output of `SecondGraphics.java`

The Main Methods of the Graphics Class

```
void setColor(Color colorObject);
void setFont(Font fontObject);
void drawString(String, s, int x, int y)
void drawLine(int startX, int startY, int endX, int endY);
void drawRect (int top, int left, int width, int height);
void fillRect(int top, int left, int width, int height);
void drawRoundRect(int top, int left, int width, int height, int diamX, int
void fillRoundRect(int top, int left, int width, int height, int diamX, int
void drawOval(int top, int left, int width, int height);
void fillOval(int top, int left, int width, int height);
void drawPolygon(int x[], int y[], int numberOfPoints);
void fillPolygon(int x[], int y[], int numberOfPoints);
void drawArc(int top, int left, int width, int height, int start, int sweep);
void fillArc(int top, int left, int width, int height, int start, int sweep);
```

Chapter 7 Exercises

1. Write a program which will show four green balls of radius 20 pixels at the corners of a square of side 150 pixels in a Frame of size 400 x 400.

2. Write a program which will write your name in large letters (use a 16 point bold font) in orange on 20 lines of a window of dimensions 500 x 500. The background color is lightGray.

3. Write a program in a frame of size 800 x 800 which will show the word 'JAVA' in the centre of the top line in "Arial" bold font size 12. On the next 8 lines, the word appears in increasingly larger sizes until it is of size 36 on the last line. The words should be symmetrical between the edges of the frame.

4. Write a program which will show the French flag - vertical rectangular bands of blue, white and red.

5. Use the basic `Graphics` methods to draw a stylized domestic scene of a house with a door and two windows, a fence at the back and a tree behind.

6. Write a simple program using `Graphics` commands to show concentric discs of random colors with radii varying from 10 to 100 pixels in steps of 10 pixels, centered at the point (250,250) relative to a `Frame` of size 500 x 500.

7. Write a program to draw a 10 x 10 grid of lines in `blue` on a `white` background. Each grid is of size 40 x 40 beginning at the upper left hand corner at point (50,50). In the center of each cell of the grid is a randomly colored disk of radius 20 pixels.

8. Write a simple graphics program which will display a circular 'wheel' of radius 150 pixels with a 5-pixel outer rim colored `darkGray`. The interior of the wheel has 30 degree sectors of different random colors. No two adjacent sectors may have the same color.

9. Write a program which will display a mosaic made up of regular hexagonal 'tiles' alternately colored `red` and `pink` on the first row and 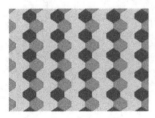 then `lightGray` and `darkGray` on the second line, then back to red and pink and so on. The side of the hexagon is of size 48 pixels. The overall size of the mosaic is such that there are ten full tiles in a row. Parts of tiles at the edges are also colored in sequence.

10. Write a graphics program to produce a picture of the flag of the United States, the Star Spangled Banner, as shown. Work out how you can save the output in a file called 'USA.JPG'. It will be used in Chapter 14. – The Swing Classes

Chapter 8   Window-, Mouse- and Keyboard Events

Events, Interfaces and Adapters

We need to be able to control the Window. At the moment we have no way of terminating a graphics program except by minimizing the window and then pressing CTRL/C to return the user to the *Command Line* prompt. Better would be if we could click on the 'X' corner button to close the window. We also also want to add keyboard and mouse controls to our programs.

A click on the window-closing button, the click or drag of a mouse, a keystroke – all these are ' events'. Every event is monitored by an object called a 'listener'. If a listener is added to the program, it will listen out for the event it is responsible for and then perform the action assigned to it by the program.

Listeners are interfaces, a sort of abstract class which does not have methods with code. The code has to be entered by the programmer to suit their program requirements. There are four main event handlers, called 'adapters' for window, mouse and keyboard events. The `WindowAdapter` responds to requests to change the shape and visibility of the window. The `MouseAdapter` responds to discrete clicks of the mouse. The `MouseMotionAdapter` is for pulling and dragging the mouse across the screen. The `KeyboardAdapter` records key presses. There are other listeners but the Adapter classes have been defined to simplify the programming of these common events.

They are all `import`'ed from the package `java.awt.event.*`.

The class `WindowAdapter`

The abstract class `WindowAdapter` has seven methods covering the different responses when a window's control buttons are pressed. These are located in the top right hand corner of the Windows screen. The complete set of actions to control the window is :

```
void windowActivated(WindowEvent wE);
void windowClosed(WindowEvent wE);
void windowClosing(WindowEvent wE);
void windowDeactivated(WindowEvent wE);
void windowIconified(WindowEvent wE);
void windowDeiconified(WindowEvent wE);
void windowOpened(WindowEvent wE);
```

For simplicity's sake we will modify only one of them. We need to be able to terminate and exit the program cleanly during program development.

To do this, we extend the class `WindowAdapter` by overriding its `windowClosing` method with one of our own. The other six abstract methods can be ignored – we don't want to do anything special with them. The class which modifies `WindowAdapter` and which we have called `MyWindowAdapter`, is shown in Fig 8.1.

`MyWindowAdapter.java` is declared public so that it can be compiled to a class file separately, after which it will be available to all our programs. All it does is terminate and exit the current program and return the user to the *Command Line* prompt when the `Frame` is closed.

```
import java.awt.event.*;
public class MyWindowAdapter extends WindowAdapter {
  public void windowClosing(WindowEvent we){
    System.exit(0);
  }
}
```

Fig 8.1 `MyWindowAdapter.java`

We can incorporate the new method for `windowClosing` in a graphics program by adding the line

```
addWindowListener(new MyWindowAdapter());
```

to the class constructor of the program..

The class MouseAdapter

To use the mouse, you have to use the MouseAdapter class which has five methods provided by the MouseListener interface. These are called

```
void mouseClicked(MouseEvent mE);
void mouseEntered(MouseEvent mE);
void mouseExited(MouseEvent mE);
void mousePressed(MouseEvent mE);
void mouseReleased(MouseEvent mE);
```

If you are only interested in the mouseClicked event, then you could extract it from the parent Adapter class by developing the following code.

```
import java.awt.event.*;
class MyMouseAdapter extends MouseAdapter{
  public void mouseClicked(MouseEvent mE) {
    . . . . . . . . . . . . . . . . .
  }
}
```

The MouseEvent class has two methods to return the screen co-ordinates of the point where the mouse is clicked. They are

```
int getX(); and    int getY();
```

We are now in a position to use the mouse inside our graphics programs. As with WindowAdapter above, we need to add a mouse listener command to the graphics program constructor. The following program, Fig 8.2, shows how. It is a simple program to display lines on a screen one after the other, each line picking up its start point from the end point of the previous line.

There are a number of important points to be noted about this program. First, you will see that the class MyWindowAdapter has been added to the constructor so that the program will close when we click on the corner 'X' button.

The class which listens for the mouse clicks is not compiled separately as a public class. Instead we must incorporate it into our program as an inner 'private class' which we could call `MyMouseAdapter`. We cannot use an external class for doing this because we need to use the (x,y) mouse position values inside our own program. The inner class is declared `private` because it is not going to be visible to classes outside the class containing it. But its methods are `public` so that they can be seen by the containing main program. The mouse listener is added to the program constructor by the instruction

```
addMouseListener(new MyMouseAdapter());
```

The method `paint(Graphics g)` is called automatically by the constructor of `Frame`. It 'paints' the initial state of the program. If we need to make a change to the screen appearance after a click of the mouse the constructor is not recalled. Therefore, we must use the command `repaint()` which redraws the screen with the updated values of the variables used to paint the screen objects.

The variable `Dimension d` defines the screen dimensions. We can reset the screen to its previous dimensions using the `getSize()` and `setSize()`. If we don't do this then minimizing the `Frame` to the Task Bar and then restoring it to full size will cause the `Frame` to fill the entire screen and its original dimensions will be lost.

The program draws a straight line between two screen locations defined by mouse clicks. The line is defined by `(x1,y1)` and `(x2,y2)` which are changed every time we click the mouse.

```
import java.awt.*;
import java.awt.event.*;
public class DrawingLinesWithMouseVersion1 extends Frame{
   Dimension d;
   int x1,x2,y1,y2;
   Font f;
   public DrawingLinesWithMouseVersion1(){
```

```
    setSize(800,600);
    d = getSize();
    setLayout(null);
    setBackground(Color.white);
    setForeground(Color.black);
    setTitle("Using the mouse to draw lines");
    setVisible(true);
    Font f = new Font("Arial",Font.BOLD,48);
    setFont(f);
    addWindowListener(new MyWindowAdapter());
    addMouseListener(new MyMouseAdapter());
  }
  private class MyMouseAdapter extends MouseAdapter{
    public void mouseClicked(MouseEvent mE)  {
      int mouseX = mE.getX();
      int mouseY = mE.getY();
      x1 = x2;
      y1 = y2;
      x2 = mouseX;
      y2 = mouseY;
      repaint();
    }
  }
  public void paint(Graphics g){
    g.drawString
      ("Fig 8.3 Drawing Lines with the mouse", 50,100);
    g.drawLine(x1,y1,x2,y2);
    setSize(d);
  }
  public static void main(String[] args){
    DrawingLinesWithMouseVersion1 dLM1 =
            new DrawingLinesWithMouseVersion1();
  }
}
```

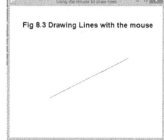

Fig 8.2 Using a Mouse Listener

The next program is a variant of the line drawing program. This time, the lines do not disappear with each click. To make this happen, we

Java Quick and Easy

have to create arrays to hold the co-ordinates of the points and an index to track the number of vertices. This program also lists the co-ordinates of the vertices down the left-hand side of the screen.

```java
import java.awt.*;
import java.awt.event.*;
public class DrawingLinesWithMouseVersion2 extends Frame{
  Dimension d;
  int[] x = new int[100];
  int[] y = new int[100];
  int index = 0;
  public DrawingLinesWithMouseVersion2(){
    setSize(600,600);
    d = getSize();
    setLayout(null);
    setBackground(Color.white);
    setForeground(Color.black);
    setTitle("Using the mouse to draw lines");
    setVisible(true);
    addWindowListener(new MyWindowAdapter());
    addMouseListener(new MyMouseAdapterModified());
  }
  private class MyMouseAdapter extends MouseAdapter{
    public void mouseClicked(MouseEvent mE) {
      int mouseX = mE.getX();
      int mouseY = mE.getY();
      x[index] = mouseX;
      y[index] = mouseY;
      index++;
      repaint();
    }
  }
  public void paint(Graphics g){
    if (index > 0){  // No numbers before a mouse click
      g.drawString(Integer.toString(0),20,50);
      g.drawString(Integer.toString(x[0]),50,50);
      g.drawString(Integer.toString(y[0]),80,50);
    }
    for (int i = 1; i<index; i++){
      g.drawLine(x[i-1],y[i-1],x[i],y[i]);
      g.drawString(Integer.toString(i),20,50+i*12);
      g.drawString(Integer.toString(x[i]),50,50+i*12);
      g.drawString(Integer.toString(y[i]),80,50+i*12);
    }
```

```
    setSize(d);
  }
  public static void main(String[] args){
    DrawingLinesWithMouseVersion2 dLM2 = new
           DrawingLinesWithMouseVersion2();
  }
}
```

Fig 8.4 `DrawingLinesWithMouseVersion2.java`

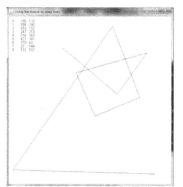

Fig 8.5 The Output of
`DrawingLinesWithMouseVersion2.java`

The class `MouseMotionAdapter`

The `MouseMotionAdapter` class is used to detect when the mouse is being dragged or moved. It has two methods.

```
void mouseDragged(MouseEvent mE);
void mouseMoved(MouseEvent mE);.
```

The same two methods of `MouseEvent` are available i.e.

```
int.getX(); and int getY();
```

Motion is monitored by the `private class MouseMotionAdapter` as an inner private class with one method, `MouseDragged`, which monitors the mouse position while the left button is pressed. It returns the mouse co-ordinates while the button is being held down. The straight line from (100,100) to (500,500) is dragged to a new shape.

```java
import java.awt.*;
import java.awt.event.*;
public class DrawingLinesWithMouseMotion extends Frame{
  Dimension d;
  int xM = 200;
  int yM = 200;
  public DrawingLinesWithMouseMotion(){
    setSize(600,600);
    d = getSize();
    setLayout(null);
    setBackground(Color.white);
    setForeground(Color.black);
    setTitle("Pulling lines out of shape");
    setVisible(true);
    addWindowListener(new MyWindowAdapter());
    addMouseMotionListener(new MyMouseMotionAdapter());
  }
  private class MyMouseMotionAdapter extends
                                    MouseMotionAdapter{
    public void mouseDragged(MouseEvent mE) {
      xM = mE.getX();
      yM = mE.getY();
      repaint();
    }
  }
  public void paint(Graphics g){
    g.drawLine(100,100,xM,yM);
    g.drawLine(xM,yM,500,500);
    setSize(d);
  }
  public static void main(String[] args){
    DrawingLinesWithMouseMotion dLMM =
                    new DrawingLinesWithMouseMotion();
  }
}
```

Fig 8.6 Using Mouse Dragging

The line is pulled out of shape by placing the cursor on the line and dragging it to the new position.

Fig 8.7 Output of
`DrawingLinesWithMouseMotion.java`

Here is another example of the use of `MouseMotionAdapter`. In this program, the user can draw freehand lines across the screen as long as the mouse's left button is held down.

```
import java.awt.*;
import java.awt.event.*;
public class DrawFreehand extends Frame{
  int[] x = new int[10000];
  int[] y = new int[10000];
  int index = 0;
  public DrawFreehand(){
    setSize(600,600);
    setLayout(null);
    setBackground(Color.white);
    setForeground(Color.black);
    setTitle("Freehand Drawing");
    setVisible(true);
    addWindowListener(new MyWindowAdapter());
    addMouseMotionListener(new MyMouseMotionAdapter());
  }

 private class MyMouseMotionAdapter extends
                                MouseMotionAdapter{
    public void mouseDragged(MouseEvent mE) {
      x[index] = mE.getX();
      y[index] = mE.getY();
      index++;
      repaint();
    }
  }
}
```

```
public void paint(Graphics g){
  for (int i = 1; i < index; i++){
    g.drawLine(x[i],y[i],x[i-1],y[i-1]);
  }
}
public static void main(String[] args){
  DrawFreehand dF = new DrawFreehand();
}
}
```

Fig 8.8 Drawing Freehand

Fig 8.9 Drawing Freehand using `MouseMotionAdapter`

The class KeyAdapter

Another important adapter class is `KeyAdapter` which recognises keystrokes from the keyboard. There are three methods

```
void keyPressed(KeyEvent kE);
void keyReleased(KeyEvent kE);
void keyTyped(KeyEvent kE);
```

Java Quick and Easy

The `KeyEvent` class has two methods:

`char getKeyChar();` and `int getKeyCode();`

These two methods return the ASCII character associated with the pressed key and its numeric value respectively. The following program shows the use of `KeyAdapter`. It returns the key codes and character values as keys are pressed.

```java
import java.awt.*;
import java.awt.event.*;
public class KeyStrokes extends Frame{
  Dimension d;
  char keyCharacter;
  int  keyCode;
  int  col = 0;
  int  row = 0;
  String s = " ";
  String s1 = " ";
  Font f1;

  public KeyStrokes(){
    setSize(700,300);
    d = getSize();
    setLayout(null);
    setBackground(Color.white);
    setForeground(Color.black);
    setTitle("Showing Key Strokes and Fonts Version 2");
    setVisible(true);
    addWindowListener(new MyWindowAdapter());
    addKeyListener(new MyKeyAdapterModified());
    f1 = new Font("Verdana", Font.BOLD, 28);
  }

  private class MyKeyAdapter extends KeyAdapter{
    public void keyPressed(KeyEvent kE) {
      keyCharacter = kE.getKeyChar();
      keyCode = kE.getKeyCode();
      s1 = s.replace(' ',keyCharacter);
      repaint();
    }
  }
}
```

```
    public void paint(Graphics g){
      g.setFont(f1);
      g.drawString
            ("Keys Pressed and Character Codes",50,100);
      g.drawString(s1,200,150);
      g.drawString(Integer.toString(keyCode),250,150);
      setSize(d);
    }
    public static void main(String[] args){
      KeyStrokes kS = new KeyStrokes();
    }
}
```

Fig 8.10 The `KeyStrokes.java` *Program*

The next program shows how to use a special key to halt a process. This program covers the window with an array of red, then blue, then red disks *etc.* The ESC key, *keyCode* number 27, halts the process. The method

`void time(long counter)`

is a simple delay device to stop the program running too quickly.

```
import java.awt.*;
import java.awt.event.*;
public class RedAndBlueDisks extends Frame{
  Dimension d;
  int   keyCode = 0;
  char keyCharacter;
  Font f1;
  int count = 0;
  String s = " ";
  String s1 = " ";
  public RedAndBlueDisks(){
    setSize(750,800);
    d = getSize();
    setLayout(null);
    setBackground(Color.white);
    setForeground(Color.black);
    setTitle("Red and blue disks");
    setVisible(true);
```

```
      addWindowListener(new MyWindowAdapter());
      addKeyListener(new MyKeyAdapter());
      f1 = new Font("Sans Serif", Font.BOLD,18);
   }
   private class MyKeyAdapter extends KeyAdapter{
      public void keyPressed(KeyEvent kE) {
         keyCode = kE.getKeyCode();
      }
   }
   void time(long counter){
      for (int i = 0; i < counter; i++){}
      repaint();
   }
   public void paint(Graphics g){
      g.setColor(Color.black);
      g.setFont(f1);
      g.drawString("Drawing continues until " +
            "ESC key (code = 27) is pressed.",60,50);
      if (count%2 == 0) {
         g.setColor(Color.red);
      }
      else
      {
         g.setColor(Color.blue);
      }
      count++;
      for (int row = 0; row < 32; row++){
         for (int col = 0; col < 36; col++) {
            if (keyCode != 27){
               g.fillOval(20*col + 20,20*row + 80, 10,10);
               time(1000000);
            }
         }
      }
      g.setColor(Color.black);
      g.drawString(Integer.toString(keyCode),700,750);
      setSize(d);
   }

   public static void main(String[] args){
      RedAndBlueDisks rBD = new RedAndBlueDisks();
   }
}
```

Fig 8.11 Using the ESC Key to Stop a Program

The output of `RedAndBlueDisks.java` is not very interesting, simply changing screens of `red` and `blue` dots, terminated by the ESC character.

The next program combines the `KeyAdapter` with the `MouseAdapter` (plus the `WindowAdapter`) to read a character from the keyboard and place it on the screen at a point defined by a mouse click.

```java
import java.awt.*;
import java.awt.event.*;
public class  PlaceChar extends Frame{
  char keyCharacter;
  Font f1;
  String s = "";
  int x,y;
  public PlaceChar(){
    setSize(600,600);
    setLayout(null);
    setBackground(Color.white);
    setForeground(Color.black);
    setTitle("Key Press and Screen"
             + " Position Defined by Mouse Click");
    setVisible(true);
    addMouseListener(new MyMouseAdapter());
    addKeyListener(new MyKeyAdapter());
    addWindowListener(new MyWindowadapter());
    f1 = new Font("Sans Serif", Font.BOLD,48);
    setFont(f1);
  }
  private class MyKeyAdapter extends KeyAdapter{
    public void keyPressed(KeyEvent kE) {
      keyCharacter = kE.getKeyChar();
      s = "";
      s = s + keyCharacter;
    }
  }
  private class MyMouseAdapter extends MouseAdapter{
    public void mouseClicked(MouseEvent mE){
      x = mE.getX();
      y = mE.getY();
      repaint();
    }
  }
```

```
public void paint(Graphics g){
  g.drawString(s,x,y);
}
public static void main(String[] args){
  PlaceChar pC = new PlaceChar();
}
}
```

Fig 8.12 A Program with
three Adapter classes

Chapter 8 Exercises

1. Write a program to create a reusable program `MyWindowAdapter` which exits the program as the 'X' corner control button is pressed. Before the Window closes, it briefly displays a message "Goodbye!" in the top left hand corner of the screen.

2. Write a program to click a mouse on the screen. Return a large red 'X' at the point where the mouse is clicked. Adjust the position so that the mouse co-ordinates coincide with the center of the 'X'

3. Modify the program in Question 2 so that if you click on an existing point within the 'X', then that point will be removed from the set of points.

4. Write a program to enter keystrokes from the keyboard and return their key code and character value in columns of 20 items on the graphics `Frame`. Put a heading on the frame 'Key Stroke Test'. Use a bold 20 point font and make the frame size at least 500 pixels deep so that the column entries will fit on the screen. When ESC (code = 27) is pressed, the program ends with a message 'ESC key was pressed' in the screen center.

5. Write a program in a `Frame` with a blue background which allows the mouse to draw a 'trail' of `white`, six pixels wide as if the screen were being wiped by an eraser.

6. Create a Java program such that when the user clicks twice on a screen with the mouse, the program will draw two points, indicated by small black `fillOval` objects with the click point at their centers. The third click also produces a point, but it also completes a triangle of the three points which is drawn with black lines..

7. Write a program to count the number of key presses in a `String` which is input from the keyboard. Output the count to the screen using the `Graphics.drawString()` method.

8. Write a program which will input two characters from the keyboard. When the mouse is clicked on the screen, the characters are displayed at that point.

9. Write a program to generate a random character in the byte range 65 – 90 or 'A 'to 'Z'. When the program runs, the user tries to guess what the character is by pressing a key. If the guess is too high, the screen responds with a message 'Too high'. Likewise if the guess is too low, the message is 'Too low'. When the guess is right, the program writes 'Congratulations!' and returns the number of key presses the user took to guess the right answer.

10. Write a simple program to play tic-tac-toe or 'noughts and crosses' as it is sometimes called. Each player takes it in turn to click on one of the cells in the grid and a 'O' or an 'X' is drawn. The program announces the winner and draws a line through the winning cells.

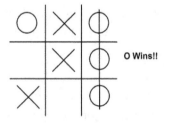

O Wins!!

Chapter 9   Programming Windows Components

The standard components of the WIMPS screen are also available through the Java Abstract Windows Toolkit. They can be combined to enable you to create a full Windows Graphical User Interface. In this chapter we look at the basic Windows objects: `Label`, `Button`, `Checkbox`, `CheckboxGroup`, `List` and `Choice`. They can be added to the `Frame` and combined with `Graphics` drawing objects on the same screen.

Label

Labels are used for displaying `String` data without using the `Graphics` method `drawString()`. The message will be displayed in the current color and font. Label has three constructors.

```
Label()
Label(String s)
Label(String s, int how);
```

The content of the `Label` is `String` `s` and the value of `how` is a constant with values `LEFT`, `CENTER`, `RIGHT` used to locate the message in the `Label` bounds.

The first one is a `Label` which starts blank and can be changed by the program. The second form is the most commonly used for text data. `Label`'s are passive so there is no event listener. `Label`'s, and all other AWT components, use the `add()` method to add the component to the `Frame`. Use

```
setBounds(x,y,width,height);
```

which is available to all Windows objects, for sizing and positioning. Here is a short program to show the use of `Label`. It adds a message in blue to a `Frame` which also has `Graphics.drawString()` and `Graphics.fillRect()` methods on it.

```java
import java.awt.*;
public class LabelDemo extends Frame {
   Label l1;
   Font f1;
   public LabelDemo(){
      setSize(500,500);
      setBackground(Color.yellow);
      setForeground(Color.blue);
      setTitle("Label Demo 1");
      setLayout(null);
      setVisible(true);
      addWindowListener(new MyWindowAdapter());
      f1 = new Font("Verdana",Font.BOLD,30);
      setFont(f1);
      l1 = new Label("This is the label");
      l1.setBounds(40,40,300,100);
      add(l1);
   }
   public void paint(Graphics g){
      g.fillRect(100,200,200,100);
      g.drawString("This is the g.drawString",40,400);
   }
   public static void main(String[] args){
      LabelDemo lD = new LabelDemo();
   }
}
```

Fig 9.1 A Simple Label Program

Fig 9.2 The Output of `LabelDemo.java`

Button

Buttons are grey boxes with a text label, usually a simple command like 'Start' or 'Cancel'. They are activated by an `ActionListener`. In the following example, an `ActionListener` variable called 'listener' is created. What the new object 'listener' does is defined by an inner class, as for `MouseAdapter` in the previous chapter. `ActionListener` is an interface, not a class, which means that it is 'implemented,' not extended. It has a single method called `actionPerformed`. The `ActionListener` is added to the Button by the instruction

```
b1.addActionListener(listener);
```

This program changes the screen color as the `Button` is pressed.

```
import java.awt.*;
import java.awt.event.*;
public class ButtonDemo extends Frame {
  Button b1;
  int index = 0;
  Font f1,f2;
    public ButtonDemo(){
    setSize(500,500);
    setBackground(Color.white);
    setForeground(Color.black);
    setTitle("Label Demo 1");
    setLayout(null);
    setVisible(true);
    f1 = new Font("Arial",Font.BOLD,24);
    f2 = new Font("Arial",Font.BOLD,48);
    addWindowListener(new MyWindowAdapter());
    ActionListener listener = new MyActionListener();
    b1 = new Button("Press me!");
    b1.setBounds(100,300,200,100);
    b1.setFont(f1);
    b1.addActionListener(listener);
    add(b1);
  }
  private class MyActionListener implements
                                  ActionListener{
    public void actionPerformed(ActionEvent aE){
```

```
      if (index%2 == 0) {
        setBackground(Color.yellow);
      }
      else
      {
        setBackground(Color.green);
      }
      index++;
    }
  }
  public void paint(Graphics g){
    g.setFont(f2);
    g.drawString("Fig 9.4",100,100);
    g.drawString("Button Demo",100,200);
  }
  public static void main(String[] args){
    ButtonDemo bD = new ButtonDemo();
  }
}
```

Fig 9.3 Using a Button to Change Screen Background Color

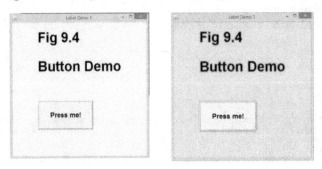

Fig 9.4 The Output of `ButtonDemo.java`

Checkbox

The single `Checkbox` has five constructors. They are

```
Checkbox();
Checkbox(String s);
Checkbox(String s, boolean on);
Checkbox(String s, boolean on ,CheckboxGroup cbGroup);
Checkbox(String s, CheckboxGroup cbGroup, boolean on);
```

92

The first constructor is a single square `Checkbox`. `String s` is the label attached to it and the `boolean` 'on' indicates whether the `Checkbox` is checked or not. (Checked is `true`.) The last two constructors attach a `Checkbox` to a `CheckboxGroup`, covered in the next section. A `Checkbox` operation is very simple – the box is either checked or unchecked. So the most important method of the `Checkbox` listener, `ItemListener()`, is `getState()`, a `boolean` method which returns the state of the box. The `String s` provides a simple method of labelling the `Checkbox` as an alternative to a separate `Label`.

The next program shows the use of the single `Checkbox`. The program does nothing more than change the background color of the screen depending on the state of the `Checkbox` exactly as for `ButtonDemo.java` above (Figs 9.3 and 9.4)

```
import java.awt.*;
import java.awt.event.*;
public class CheckboxDemo extends Frame {
Checkbox c1;
  public CheckboxDemo(){
    setSize(500,500);
    setBackground(Color.white);
    setForeground(Color.black);
    setTitle("Checkbox Demo 1");
    setLayout(null);
    setVisible(true);
    addWindowListener(new MyWindowAdapter());
    ItemListener listener = new MyItemListener();
    c1 = new Checkbox("Tick me!");
    c1.setBounds(250,250,100,40);
    c1.addItemListener(listener);
    add(c1);
  }
  private class MyItemListener implements ItemListener{
  boolean ticked = true;
    public void itemStateChanged(ItemEvent iE){
      ticked = c1.getState();
      if (ticked){
        setBackground(Color.yellow);
      }
      else
      {
```

```
        setBackground(Color.green);
      }
    }
  }
  public void paint(Graphics g){
    g.drawString("Checkbox Demo",100,100);
  }
  public static void main(String[] args){
    CheckboxDemo cD = new CheckboxDemo();
  }
}
```

Fig 9.5 The Use of a Single Checkbox

Methods of AWT Components(1)

Common AWT Methods	add();
	remove();
	setBounds(int *x0,y0,width,height*);		

Label		**Checkbox**	
Constants	LEFT, RIGHT, CENTER	*Methods*	boolean getState();

Methods	void setText(String *s*);
	String getText();
	void setAlignment(int *how*);
	int getAlignment();
			void setState(boolean *on*);
			String getLabel();
			void setLabel(String *s*);

		Listener	ItemListener
Button			
Methods	void setLabel(String *s*); String getLabel();		
Listener	ActionListener		

CheckboxGroup

If the user of the program needs to make a single choice from several, then a CheckboxGroup is one way to do it. In Java, multiple Checkbox's which are grouped change their shape from square to round and are often called 'radio buttons'. Each Checkbox (or radio button) in the group is added separately to the Window and each must have the same ActionListener. The following short program shows how to create a CheckboxGroup. The program is very simple – it merely presents a group of three boxes labelled 'A', 'B' and 'C' and returns the letter of the Checkbox which has been chosen.

```java
import java.awt.*;
import java.awt.event.*;
public class CheckboxGroupDemo extends Frame {
  Checkbox c1,c2,c3,cWhich;
  CheckboxGroup cbg;
  boolean b1,b2,b3;
  boolean chosen = false;
  String s1 = "";
  Font f = new Font("Arial",Font.BOLD,28);
  Font f1 = new Font("Arial",Font.BOLD,36);
  public CheckboxGroupDemo(){
    setSize(600,500);
    setBackground(Color.yellow);
    setForeground(Color.black);
    setTitle("Check Box Group Demo");
    setLayout(null);
    setVisible(true);
    addWindowListener(new MyWindowAdapter());
    ItemListener listener = new MyItemListener();
    cbg = new CheckboxGroup();
    c1 = new Checkbox("A",cbg,false);
    c1.setBounds(100,150,100,40);
    c1.setFont(f);
    c1.addItemListener(listener);
    c2 = new Checkbox("B",cbg,false);
    c2.setBounds(100,200,100,40);
    c2.setFont(f);
    c2.addItemListener(listener);
    c3 = new Checkbox("C",cbg,false);
    c3.setBounds(100,250,100,40);
    c3.setFont(f);
    c3.addItemListener(listener);
    add(c1);
    add(c2);
    add(c3);
  }

  private class MyItemListener implements ItemListener{
    public void itemStateChanged(ItemEvent iE){
      chosen = true;
      cWhich = cbg.getSelectedCheckbox();
      s1 = cWhich.getLabel();
      repaint();
    }
  }
}
```

```
public void paint(Graphics g){
  g.setFont(f1);
  g.drawString(" Fig 9.8 CheckboxGroup Demo",40,100);
  if (chosen){
    g.drawString("You chose " + s1,100,350);
  }
}
public static void main(String[] args){
  CheckboxGroupDemo cbGD = new CheckboxGroupDemo();
}
}
```

Fig 9.6 `CheckboxGroupDemo.java` *showing 'Radio' Buttons*

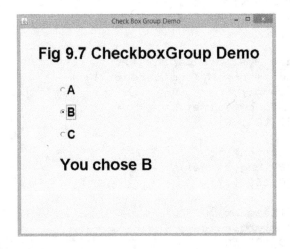

Fig 9.7 The Output of `CheckboxGroupDemo.java`

Choice

Pull-down `Choice` lists allow you to choose a single item from a selection of possibilities. They also use the `ItemListener` interface. Each item in the `Choice` list needs to be added to it separately as in the following example which selects a season from a pull-down `Choice`.

```
import java.awt.*;
import java.awt.event.*;
public class ChoiceDemo extends Frame {
```

```
  Choice season;
  String s;
  Font f,f1;
  public ChoiceDemo(){
    setSize(500,500);
    setBackground(Color.lightGray);
    setForeground(Color.black);
    setTitle("Pull Down Choice Demo");
    setLayout(null);
    setVisible(true);
    f = new Font("Arial",Font.BOLD,24);
    f1 = new Font("Arial",Font.BOLD,36);
    addWindowListener(new MyWindowAdapter());
    season = new Choice();
    season.add("Spring");
    season.add("Summer");
    season.add("Autumn");
    season.add("Winter");
    season.select("Spring");
    season.setBounds(100,200,250,70);
    season.setFont(f);
    ItemListener listener = new MyItemListener();
    season.addItemListener(listener);
    add(season);
  }
  private class MyItemListener implements ItemListener{
    public void itemStateChanged(ItemEvent iE){
      repaint();
    }
  }
  public void paint(Graphics g){
    g.setFont(f1);
    g.drawString("Fig 9.11 Choice Demo",50,100);
    g.drawString("Current season chosen is ",50,400);
    s = season.getSelectedItem();
    g.drawString(s,200,450);
  }
  public static void main(String[] args){
    ChoiceDemo cD = new ChoiceDemo();
  }
}
```

Fig 9.8 Using ChoiceDemo.java

Fig 9.9 The Output of `ChoiceDemo.java`

List

The `List` is very similar to `Choice` with the difference that it allows for multiple selections. The `List` constructors are

```
List()
List(int numberOfRows);
List(int numberOfRows, boolean permitMultipleSelect);
```

The first two are for single selection only. Multiple selections are possible by setting `permitMultipleSelect` to `true`. The number of rows in the `List` can also be set by the `int` argument. The other methods of `List` follow those of `Choice` above. Here is a simple program showing how to use the multiple selection functionality of the pull-down list.

```java
import java.awt.*;
import java.awt.event.*;
public class ListDemo extends Frame {
  List month;
  String s;
  Font f,f1;
  public ListDemo(){
    setSize(500,750);
    setBackground(Color.lightGray);
    setForeground(Color.black);
    setTitle("Pull Down List Demo");
    setLayout(null);
    setVisible(true);
    month = newList(12,true);
    month.add("January");
    month.add("February");
    month.add("March");
    month.add("April");
    month.add("May");
    month.add("June");
    month.add("July");
    month.add("August");
    month.add("September");
    month.add("October");
    month.add("November");
    month.add("December");
    month.setBounds(50,200,200,40);
    month.setFont(f);
    ItemListener listener = new MyItemListener();
    month.addItemListener(listener);
    f = new Font("Arial",Font.BOLD,28);
    f1 = new Font("Arial",Font.BOLD,36);
    addWindowListener(new MyWindowAdapter());
    add(month);
  }

  private class MyItemListener implements ItemListener{
    public void itemStateChanged(ItemEvent iE){
      repaint();
    }
  }

  public void paint(Graphics g){
    int selection[];
    g.setFont(f1);
    g.drawString("Fig 9.13 List Demo",50,100);
```

```
    s = "Months selected are : ";
    g.drawString(s,50,300);
    selection = month.getSelectedIndexes();
    for (int i = 0; i < selection.length; i++){
      g.drawString
        (month.getItem(selection[i]),50,350+i*30);
    }
  }

  public static void main(String[] args){
    ListDemo cD = new ListDemo();
  }
}
```

Fig 9.10 Multiple Choices from a List

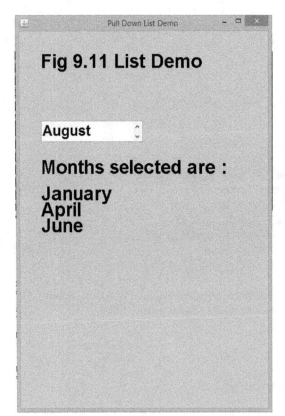

Fig 9.11 Output of
ListDemo.java

Methods of AWT Components(2)

CheckboxGroup		List	
Methods	Checkbox getSelectedCheckbox();	*Methods*	void add(String *name*);
	void setSelectedCheckbox(Checkbox *which*);		*Index*);
Listener	ItemListener		String getSelectedItem();
			int getSelectedIndex();
Choice			String[] getSelectedItem ();
Methods	void addItem(String *name*);		int[] getSelectedIndex();
	add(String *name*);		int getItemCount();
	String getSelectedItem();		void select(int *Index*);
	Int getSelectedIndex();		String getItem(int *Index*);
	int getItemCount();	*Listener*	ActionListener
	void select(int *Index*);		
	void select(String *name*);		
	String getItem(int *index*);		
Listener	ItemListener		

Chapter 9 Exercises

1. Write a program which puts a Label "JAVA QUICK AND EASY!!" on to a Frame in large blue letters, on a red background.

2. Modify the program in Q.1 above by adding a MouseAdapter. Clicking the mouse on the screen determines where the Label will be placed.

3. Modify the program in Question 1 above to display a vertical column of six Label's in random colors on the left of the screen. The font types are also randomly chosen and the size of the message varies from 12 point, by steps of 4 up to 36 point.

4. Add a Button to the program in Question 1 above so that each time you press it, the background color goes from blue to red and back again alternately.

5. Imagine your Frame is a key input into which you must enter a code. Write a program to put ten square Button's numbered '0' to '9' and enter a four-digit number. As you enter each digit, the number is displayed below the line of Button's.

Java Quick and Easy

6. Put three `Button`'s named "Red", "Green", "Blue" on a `Frame` and, when they are pressed, a message shows "I am Blue!!!", etc. in its color.

Red	Green	Blue

I am Blue!!!

7. Write a program to show a named `Checkbox` in a `Frame` with the `Label` "This is my checkbox". When the box is checked, the message "Checked!!" appears at the foot of the `Frame`.

8. Write a `CheckboxGroup` program with three buttons labeled "Curly", "Larry" and "Moe". As each `Checkbox` is chosen, a message beneath them shows "You chose....." and the Stooge's name.

9. Write a program to show a `Frame` containing a single-selection `Choice` object from "Eeny". "Meeny", "Miney" and "Mo". Your `Choice` selection will be printed beneath the list. It may be removed by pressing a `Button` marked "Clear".

10. Draw a `Frame` with three pull-down single selection `Choice`'s for "Date of Birth". The choices are labeled "Day", "Month" and "Year". Return the final date value in suitable format when you press a `Button`.

11. Create a program with a pull-down `List` allowing multiple selections from it. The `Label` of the `List` is 'Choose first name' and the `List` entries are Andrew, Brian, Charles, David, Edward, Francis. Write the choice of names below the `List`.

Chapter 10 More Components of the AWT

TextField

A TextField is a small box where String data can be entered in a GUI. It is an important part of Windows program design as the main method for entering data to the program. Its constructors are:

```
TextField();
TextField(int numberOfCharsWide);
TextField(String initialString);
TextField(String initialString,int numberOfCharsWide);
```

It uses standard methods for handling text

```
String s = getText();   void setText(String s);
```

Text can be in variable font or color.

In the next program, a simple interface requests a name and password and returns the input values to the output screen. The password can be made unreadable by replacing visible characters with an echo character using

```
setEchoChar(char echoChar);
```

The ActionListener listens for a CRLF character to terminate the entry of characters into the TextField box.

```
import java.awt.*;
import java.awt.event.*;
public class TextFieldDemo extends Frame {
  TextField name, password;
  Label l1,l2;
  public TextFieldDemo(){
    setSize(1000,800);
    setLayout(null);
    setForeground(Color.blue);
    setBackground(Color.white);
```

```
    setTitle("TextField Demo");
    setVisible(true);
    l1 = new Label("Name : ");
    l2 = new Label("Password : ");
    l1.setBounds(20,100,70,40);
    l2.setBounds(20,150,70,40);
    name = new TextField(12);
    password = new TextField(8);
    password.setEchoChar('*');
    name.setBounds(100,100,150,20);
    password.setBounds(100,150,150,20);
    add(l1);
    add(l2);
    add(name);
    add(password);
    name.addActionListener(new MyActionListener());
    password.addActionListener(new MyActionListener());
    addWindowListener(new MyWindowAdapter());
  }
  private class MyActionListener implements
                                  ActionListener{
    public void actionPerformed(ActionEvent aE){
      repaint();
    }
  }
  public void paint(Graphics g){
    g.setColor(Color.black);
    g.drawString("TextField Demo",20,50);
    g.drawString("Name is " + name.getText(), 20, 250);
    g.drawString("Password is "+
                            password.getText(),20,300);
  }
  public static void main(String[] args){
    TextFieldDemo tFD = new
TextFieldDemo();
  }
}
```

Fig 10.1 Using a `TextField`

ig 10.2 The Output of
TextFieldDemo.java

TextField Demo

TextField Demo

Name : Chris Payne

Password : ************

Name is Chris Payne

Password is 1QEs56HePl73

Java Quick and Easy

TextArea

Sometimes larger sets of character data need to be entered, for which a `TextArea` can be used. `TextArea` has no `ActionListener` of its own, so some other event handler such as a `Button` must be added before the program can use the input. If the amount of data to be input exceeds the `TextArea` dimensions, then scroll bars appear to extend the input area.. The following program illustrates the use of `TextArea`.

```java
import java.awt.*;
import java.awt.event.*;
public class TextAreaDemo extends Frame {
  TextArea tA;
  Button b1;
  String s = "";
  public TextAreaDemo() {
    setSize(1000,800);
    setLayout(null);
    setForeground(Color.blue);
    setBackground(Color.white);
    setTitle("TextArea Demo");
    setVisible(true);
    tA = new TextArea();
    tA.setBounds(20,100,250,200);
    b1 = new Button("End Input");
    b1.setBounds(20,350,100,40);
    addWindowListener(new MyWindowAdapter());
    b1.addActionListener(new MyActionListener());
    add(b1);
    add(tA);
  }
  private class MyActionListener implements
                              ActionListener{
    public void actionPerformed(ActionEvent aE) {
      s = tA.getText();
      repaint();
    }
  }
  public void paint(Graphics g) {
    Font f = new Font("Arial", Font.BOLD, 24);
    g.setColor(Color.black);
    g.setFont(f);
    g.drawString("TextArea Demo",50,60);
```

```
    g.drawString(s,20,450);
  }
  public static void main(String[] args){
    TextAreaDemo tAD = new TextAreaDemo();
  }
}
```

Fig 10.3 Using a `TextArea`

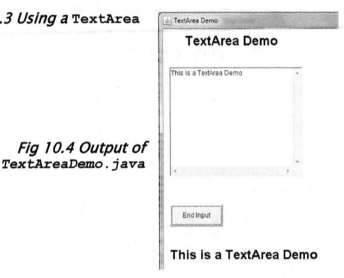

Fig 10.4 Output of
TextAreaDemo.java

Menu

Setting up a `Menu` in the AWT is a complicated multi-stage process. The actual `Menu`'s are pull-down lists attached to a `MenuBar` and each pull-down list may have numerous `MenuItem`'s.

Once the `MenuBar` is defined, we can add named `Menu`'s to it. In the following example, `MenuDemo.java`, we set up a `MenuBar` with three `Menu`'s titled 'File', 'Edit' and 'Help'. The 'File' `Menu` has five `MenuItem`'s, the 'Edit' `Menu` has three `MenuItem`'s and the 'Help' `Menu` has two.

The private class `MenuListener` implements the `ActionListener` which has an `actionPerformed` method. This method must be applied to every `MenuItem`. So that the program can distinguish which `MenuItem` is being clicked on, we must use the

`ActionEvent.getSource()` method which returns the symbolic name of the `MenuItem` we wish to activate.

```java
import java.awt.*;
import java.awt.event.*;
public class MenuDemo extends Frame {
  MenuBar menuBar = new MenuBar();
  Menu fileMenu = new Menu("File");
  Menu editMenu = new Menu("Edit");
  Menu helpMenu = new Menu("Help");
  MenuItem newMenuItem = new MenuItem("New");
  MenuItem openMenuItem = new MenuItem("Open");
  MenuItem saveMenuItem = new MenuItem("Save");
  MenuItem saveAsMenuItem = new MenuItem("Save As");
  MenuItem exitMenuItem = new MenuItem("Exit");
  MenuItem cutMenuItem = new MenuItem("Cut");
  MenuItem copyMenuItem = new MenuItem("Copy");
  MenuItem pasteMenuItem = new MenuItem("Paste");
  MenuItem helpMenuItem = new MenuItem("Online help");
  MenuItem aboutMenuItem = new MenuItem("About");
  MenuListener listener = new MenuListener();
  String s = "";
  public MenuDemo() {
    setSize(600,600);
    setLayout(null);
    setFont(new Font("Arial",Font.BOLD,16));
    setBackground(Color.lightGray);
    setForeground(Color.black);
    setTitle("Menu Demo");
    setVisible(true);
    setMenuBar(menuBar);
    menuBar.add(fileMenu);
    menuBar.add(editMenu);
    menuBar.add(helpMenu);
    fileMenu.add(newMenuItem);
    fileMenu.add(openMenuItem);
    fileMenu.add(saveMenuItem);
    fileMenu.add(saveAsMenuItem);
    fileMenu.add(exitMenuItem);
    editMenu.add(cutMenuItem);
    editMenu.add(copyMenuItem);
    editMenu.add(pasteMenuItem);
    helpMenu.add(helpMenuItem);
    helpMenu.add(aboutMenuItem);
```

```java
   newMenuItem.addActionListener(listener);
   openMenuItem.addActionListener(listener);
   saveMenuItem.addActionListener(listener);
   saveAsMenuItem.addActionListener(listener);
   exitMenuItem.addActionListener(listener);
   cutMenuItem.addActionListener(listener);
   copyMenuItem.addActionListener(listener);
   pasteMenuItem.addActionListener(listener);
   helpMenuItem.addActionListener(listener);
   aboutMenuItem.addActionListener(listener);
   addWindowListener(new MyWindowAdapter());
}
private class MenuListener implements ActionListener{
   public void actionPerformed(ActionEvent aE){
      Object source = aE.getSource();
      if (source == newMenuItem){
         s = "New";
      }
      if (source == openMenuItem){
         s = "Open";
      }
      if (source == saveMenuItem){
         s = "Save";
      }
      if (source == saveAsMenuItem){
         s = "Save As";
      }
      if (source == exitMenuItem){
         System.exit(0);
      }
     if (source == cutMenuItem){
         s = "Cut";
      }
      if (source == copyMenuItem){
         s = "Copy";
      }
      if (source == pasteMenuItem){
         s = "Paste";
      }
      if (source == helpMenuItem){
         s = "Online Help";
      }
      if (source == aboutMenuItem){
         s = "About";
      }
      repaint(0);
```

```
      }
    }
    public void paint(Graphics g) {
      g.setColor(Color.blue);
      g.setFont(new Font("Arial",Font.BOLD,48));
      g.drawString("Fig 10.6 Menu Demo",50,250);
      g.setColor(Color.black);
      g.setFont(new Font("Arial",Font.BOLD,36));
      g.drawString("You chose :",50,400);
      g.drawString(s,300,400);
    }

    public static void main(String[] args){
      MenuDemo mM = new MenuDemo();
    }
}
```

Fig 10.5 A Program to Set Up a Menu Structure

We have reduced the coding effort here by limiting the number of live `MenuItem`'s. Large `Menu`'s, each with large numbers of `MenuItem`'s can lead to a huge program. We have also not considered multi-level menus where a menu choice generates a new menu of its own.

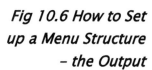

Fig 10.6 How to Set up a Menu Structure – the Output

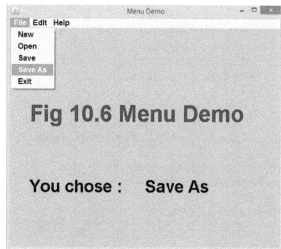

Image

There is a class, `Image`, in the AWT which allows you to import image files in standard formats – *JPG, .TIFF, .GIF, .PNG, .BMP* etc. – into your Windows programs. The program must take care of the possible `IOException` by a `try..catch` control or by declaring it thrown. Whenever an external file needs to be imported, there will always be the possibility of such an exception if the program is going to be used by a third party who may not have access to it.

To use methods for the input/output of files contining images the package `javax.imageio` must be imprted by the instruction:

```
import javax.imageio.*;
```

The first program simply imports a basic image file and displays it via `paint(Graphics g)`.

```
import java.awt.*;
import java.awt.image.*;
import javax.imageio.*;
import java.io.*;
public class FirstImage extends Frame{
  Image img;
  public FirstImage() {
    setSize(400,400);
    setLayout(null);
    setBackground(Color.white);
    setForeground(Color.black);
    setTitle('First Image');
    addWindowListener(new MyWindowAdapter());
    try{
      img = ImageIO.read(new File("FI.jpg"));
    }
    catch(IOException e){}
    setVisible(true);
  }
  public void paint(Graphics g){
    g.drawImage(img,100,100,null);
  }
  public static void main(String[] args){
```

```
    FirstImage fI = new FirstImage();
  }
}
```

Fig 10.7 The Program `FirstImage.java`

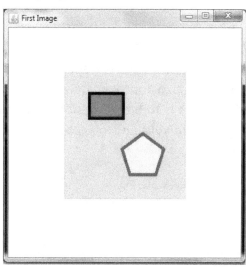

Fig 10.8 The Output of
`FirstImage.java`

A second version of the `Graphics.drawImage()` method is very useful for editing the imported images. Its form is

```
boolean Graphics.drawImage(Image img,
        int dstx1, int dsty1, int dstx2, int dsty2,
        int srcx1, int srcy1, int srcx2, int srcy2,
        ImageObserver observer);
```

The `src` parameters represent the dimensions of the source image which we are going to to copy and draw i.e the pixel values of the top left and bottom right corners of the source. The `dst` parameters display the area of the target destination where the image will be placed in the object `Frame`.

The width and height dimensions on the destination `Frame` are calculated by the expressions: `(dstx2 - dstx1)`, `(dsty2 - dsty1)`. If the dimensions of the source and destinations areas are different, Java will scale up or scale down, as needed.

In effect, this method will allow you to edit and re-size your image. The `ImageObserver` class has a single method, `imageUpdate()`, which allows you to observe the progress of an image transfer over, maybe, a network. The value of its variable, `observer`, is set to `null` for our purposes.

The following program shows how this version of `drawImage` is used. The input image file started life as a full-size photograph in *JPG* format with size approximately 2000 x 3000 pixels. The top two thirds of this image is to be reproduced. It is then reduced to an image of size 500 x 500 pixels and placed with its top left hand corner at point (100,100).

```
import java.awt.*;
import java.awt.image.*;
import javax.imageio.*;
import java.io.*;
public class SecondImage extends Frame{
  Image img;
  public SecondImage() {
    setSize(700,700);
    setLayout(null);
    setBackground(Color.white);
    setForeground(Color.black);
    setTitle('Second Image');
    addWindowListener(new MyWindowAdapter());
    try{
      img = ImageIO.read(new File("VeniceBuilding.JPG"));
    }
    catch(IOException e){}
    setVisible(true);
  }
  public void paint(Graphics g){
    g.drawImage(img,100,100,600,600,0,0,2000,2000,null);
  }
  public static void main(String[] args){
    SecondImage sI = new SecondImage();
  }
}
```

Fig 10.9 Resizing and Repositioning of an Image

Fig 10.10
The Edited Image

FileDialog Box

A Windows component which is very useful is the `FileDialog` box which is the box used to load and save files. It is a very powerful class, which does a lot in return for small number of program instructions.

    `FileDialog` has three constructors :

```
FileDialog(Frame parent,String boxName);
FileDialog(Frame parent,String boxName,int how);
FileDialog(Frame parent);
```

The `Frame` parent is the window which holds the `FileDialog` box and `boxName` is the title `String` of the box. The variable `int` how has two values:

`LOAD` opens the `FileDialog` box for reading a file
`SAVE` opens the `FileDialog` box for saving a file.

The use of the `FileDialog` class is shown in the following program. The parent `Frame` is the current instantiation of the host class.

```
import java.awt.*;
import java.awt.event.*;
public class FileDialogDemo extends Frame {
  public FileDialogDemo(){
    setSize(700,700);
    setBackground(Color.white);
    setForeground(Color.black);
    setTitle("File Dialog Demo");
    setLayout(null);
    setVisible(true);
    addWindowListener(new MyWindowAdapter());
  }
  public static void main(String[] args){
    FileDialogDemo fDD = new FileDialogDemo();
    FileDialog fd = new FileDialog(fDD,
              "File Dialog",FileDialog.SAVE);
    fd.setVisible(true);
  }
}
```

Fig 10.10 Using a `FileDialog` *Box*

The `FileDialog` class does not automatically save or load a file but instead it provides two methods, `String getDirectory()` and `String getFile()` to return the path and file name of the entry selected in the `FileDialog's` `TextField`.

Fig 10.12 Output from
`FileDialogDemo.java`

Methods of AWT Component(3)		
TextField		**TextArea**

TextField

Methods
- String getText();
- void setText(String s);
- String getSelectedText();
- void select(int startindex, int endindex);
- boolean isEditable(0;
- void setEditable(boolean canBeEdited);
- void setEchoChar(char ch);
- boolean echoCharSet();
- char getEchoChar();

Listener ActionListener

TextArea

Constants
- int SCROLLBARS_BOTH,
- int SCROLLBARS_NONE
- int SCROLLBARS_HORIZONTAL_ONLY,
- int SCROLLBARS_VERTICAL_ONLY,

Methods
- String getText();
- void setText(string s);
- String getSelectedText();
- void select(int startindex, int endindex);
- boolean isEditable(0;
- void setEditable(boolean canBeEdited);
- void append(String s);
- void insert(String s, int index);
- void replaceRange(String s, int startindex, int endindex);

Chapter 10 Exercises

1. Write a Java program which contains two `TextField`'s and two `Label`'s 'Enter amount $:' and 'Exchange Rate $:Eu:' . Enter a dollar amount and a $:Eu exchange rate and return the Euro equivalent as a `String` in `Graphics.drawString` when a `Button` 'Go' is pressed.

2. Write a Java program with a `TextArea` and a `Button` ("Go"). Data entered into the `TextArea` is written to a file when the `Button` is pressed. Read back the file and output the data to the console.

3. Write a program to show a `TextField` and a `Button` on a screen. The `TextField` also has a `Label` 'Date of birth (MM-DD-YYYY)'. When a date is entered, and the `Button` is pressed, the program returns a `Label` showing the number of days since January 1st 1900.

4. Create a simple image file using a graphics editor like Microsoft Paint and resize it to 100 x 100 pixels. Then write a Java program to 'tile' i.e. produce multiple copies of the image in a square with five per column and five per row.

5. Write a program to display a `FileDialog` box. Enter a file name and save the file to one of your directories. Check that the file has actually been added to your stored files in the correct directory.

6. Write a Java program to set up `Menu`'s on a `MenuBar` with titles 'File', 'Edit', 'View', 'Help'. The 'View' `Menu` has four items – 'Left' and 'Right', 'Hand' and 'Foot'.

7. Develop the program in Question 6 to respond to the four `MenuItem`'s in the 'View' `Menu` so that when a choice is made, a `Label` showing 'Left', or 'Right' and 'Hand' or 'Foot' appears in the center of the `Frame`.

8. Write a program to create a `Menu` structure with two `Menu`'s on a `MenuBar`. One `Menu` is called 'Input' and has `MenuItem`'s called 'Keyboard', 'Tablet', ' Mouse', 'Scanner'. the other `Menu` is called 'Output' and has `MenuItem`'s called 'Console', 'Screen', 'Printer' and 'Speaker'. As each `MenuItem` is chosen, the program outputs a `Label` with the names of the `MenuItem`'s chosen.

9. Write a program to simulate a simple calculator with two `TextField`'s separated by a `Choice` pull-down list. The program allows you to enter real numbers into the two `TextField`'s. The arithmetic operation is defined by '+', '–', '*', '/' in the `Choice` list. The program responds with the answer to the calculation in a `Label` below the `Choice`. Trap the condition where the divisor is zero.

10. Write a program to set up a GUI menu with a `MenuBar` and three `Menu`'s each holding three `MenuItem`'s. The three `Menu`'s are named 'Red', 'Green' and 'Blue'. On each `Menu` are the names of three shapes – circle, square and triangle. Selecting a `MenuItem` draws the shape in its color in the middle of the GUI screen.

Chapter 11 Animated Graphics

The Animation Cycle.

With an understanding of the methods of the AWT, it is possible to produce simple graphics animations. The basic process of creating an animated graphic is the cycle :

1. Draw the graphic
2. Delay the picture for a short time
3. Calculate the co-ordinates of the picture in a new position
4. Extinguish the picture in its old position by
          merging it with its background
5. Redraw the graphic to its new position using the
       `repaint()` method
6. Repeat steps 2–5 as required.

The basic template for a simple animation class is

```
import java.awt.*;
public class AnimationExampleProgram {
  long someLargeNumber;
  public AnimationExampleProgram() extends Frame{
    // here is where you define the frame,
  }
  void changePositionOfScreenObjects() {
             // change positions of objects on screen
    repaint(); // final instruction in this method
  }
  void delay(long time){
    for (long l = 0; l < time; l++){}
      // controls the speed of the screen objects
    }
  }
  public void paint(Graphics g){
    // paint the screen objects in the current position
    delay(someLargeNumber);
    // hold screen position for a moment
```

```
      changePositionofScreenObjects();
   }
   public static void main(String[] args){
      AnimationExampleProgram aEP =
                      new AnimationExampleProgram();
   }
}
```

Fig 11.1 The Basic Animation Program Cycle

The following program is the simplest example of animation. It merely has a red disc moving across the screen.

```
import java.awt.*;
public class FirstAnimation extends Frame{
   int x = 50;
   int y = 100;
   int diameter = 40;
   long someLargeNumber = 10000000;

   public FirstAnimation() {
      setTitle("First Animation");
      setSize(500,500);
      setBackground(Color.white);
      setLayout(null);
      setVisible(true);
   }
   void changePositionOfScreenObjects(){
      x++;
      repaint();
   }
   public void paint(Graphics g){
      g.setColor(Color.red);
      g.fillOval(x,y,diameter,diameter);
      delay(someLargeNumber);
      g.setColor(Color.white);
      changePositionOfScreenObjects();
      delay(someLargeNumber);
   }

   void delay(long time){
      for (long l = 0; l < time; l++){}
   }
```

```
public static void main(String[] args){
  FirstAnimation fA = new FirstAnimation();
 }
}
```

Fig 11.2 A Very Simple Animation Progam

The program in Fig 11.2 advances the upper left hand corner of the
`Graphics.fillOval` method in each cycle. The delay is made by
making the computer count up to a very large number as in the method
`void delay(long time)`.

Rather than writing a new program every time, one could build up a
collection of reusable graphics objects. The following class,
`DrawObjects`, shows how to do this. Four objects are defined – a car,
two tree types and a house. With imagination, it would be easy enough
to create other objects for your scene.

The methods of this class are defined by relative co-ordinates, with
relative sizes. The `drawCar` method also allows you to define the color
of the car.

The objects can be re-sized and placed in any screen location and
any number of them can be instantiated in a well-populated animation
program. This class has no `main()` method since it is intended only to
be used by other applications.

```
import java.awt.*;
public class DrawObjects{
  Graphics g;
  void drawCar(int x, int y,int l, Color c){
    /* x,y are top LH corner co-ordinates;
       l is car length, c is body color */
    int[] x0 = {x,x+1/6,x+2*1/3,x+3*1/4,x+1,x+1,x};
    int[] y0 = {y+1/4,y,y,y+1/4,y+1/3,y+1/2,y+1/2};
    int[] x1 = {x+1/20,x+11*1/60,x+1/3,x+1/3};
    int[] y1 = {y+1/4,y+1/20,y+1/20,y+1/4};
    int[] x2 = {x+23*1/60,x+23*1/60,x+19*1/30,x+7*1/10};
    int[] y2 = {y+1/4,y+1/20,y+1/20,y+1/4};
    g.setColor(c);
    g.fillPolygon(x0,y0,7);
    g.setColor(Color.black);
```

```java
        g.drawPolygon(x0,y0,7);
        g.drawLine(x+22*1/60,y,x+22*1/60,y+1/2);
        g.drawLine(x+3*1/4,y+1/4,x+3*1/4,y+1/2);
        g.setColor(Color.white);
        g.fillOval(x+3*1/4,y+3*1/8,1/4,1/4);
        g.fillOval(x+1/16,y+3*1/8,1/4,1/4);
        g.setColor(Color.black);
        g.fillOval(x+49*1/64,y+25*1/64,11*1/50,11*1/50);
        g.fillOval(x+1/13,y+25*1/64,11*1/50,11*1/50);
        g.setColor(Color.gray);
        g.fillOval(x+51*1/64,y+27*1/64,8*1/50,8*1/50);
        g.fillOval(x+21*1/200,y+27*1/64,8*1/50,8*1/50);
        g.setColor(Color.lightGray);
        g.fillPolygon(x1,y1,4);
        g.fillPolygon(x2,y2,4);
}
void drawPineTree(int x,int y,int size){
        int[] x0 = {x+size/2,x+size,x};
        int[] y0 = {y,y+2*size/3,y+2*size/3};
        g.setColor(Color.green);
        g.fillPolygon(x0,y0,3);
        g.setColor(Color.orange);
        g.fillRect(x+5*size/12,y+2*size/3,size/6,size/3);
}
void drawPoplarTree(int x,int y,int size){
        g.setColor(Color.orange);
        g.fillRect(x+size/12,y+2*size/3,size/12,size/4);
        g.setColor(Color.green);
        g.fillOval(x,y,size/4,3*size/4);
}
void drawHouse(int x, int y, int size){
        int[] x0 = {x,x+size/4,x+3*size/4,x+size};
        int[] y0 = {y,y-size/6,y-size/6,y};
        g.setColor(Color.yellow);
        g.fillRect(x,y,size,size/2);
        g.setColor(Color.lightGray);
        g.fillRect(x+size/10,y+size/10,size/5,size/5);
        g.fillRect(x+7*size/10,y+size/10,size/5,size/5);
        g.setColor(Color.blue);
        g.fillRect(x+7*size/16,y+size/8,size/8,3*size/8);
        g.setColor(Color.darkGray);
        g.fillPolygon(x0,y0,4);
        g.setColor(Color.black);
        g.drawRect(x+size/10,y+size/10,size/5,size/5);
        g.drawRect(x+7*size/10,y+size/10,size/5,size/5);
        g.drawLine(x+size/10,y+size/5,x+3*size/10,y+size/5);
```

```
    g.drawLine(x+size/5,y+size/10,x+size/5,y+3*size/10);
    g.drawLine(x+7*size/10,y+size/5,x+9*size/10,y+size/5);
    g.drawLine(x+4*size/5,y+size/10,x+4*size/5,
                                          y+3*size/10);
    g.setColor(Color.red);
    g.fillRect(x+3*size/4,y-size/4,size/10,size/5);
  }
}
```

Fig 11.3   A Class of Drawable Objects

Once we have this class of drawable object methods, they can be used
in a graphical program such as this one, which is called
ImportDraw.java. It shows a stylized scene across which passes a
stream of different colored cars.

```
import java.awt.*;
import java.awt.event.*;
public class ImportDraw extends Frame {
  int x = 0;
  int y = 400;
  int index = 0;
  DrawObjects dO;
  Color c = Color.blue;
  Button b;
  public ImportDraw(){
    dO = new DrawObjects();
    setSize(1000,1000);
    setBackground(Color.white);
    setForeground(Color.black);
    setTitle("Import drawing objects");
    setLayout(null);
    setVisible(true);
    ActionListener listener = new MyListener();
    b = new Button("Finish");
    b.setBounds(900,940,90,40);
    b.addActionListener(listener);
    add(b);
    addWindowListener(new MyWindowAdapter());
  }
  private class MyListener implementsActionListener{
    public void actionPerformed(ActionEvent aE){
      System.exit(0);
    }
```

```
}
void delay(long time){
  for (long l = 0; l<time; l++){}
}
void changePosition(int inX, int inY){
  int colorIndex = 0;
  x++;
  if (x == 1100){
    x = 0;
    index++;
    colorIndex = index%5;
    switch(colorIndex){
      case(0):c = Color.blue; break;
      case(1):c = Color.red; break;
      case(2):c = Color.green; break;
      case(3):c = Color.gray; break;
      case(4):c = Color.black;
    }
  }
  if (x%2 == 0){
    y = y+2;
  }
  else
  {
    y = y-2;
  }
  repaint();
}
public void paint(Graphics g){
  dO.g = g;
  g.setColor(Color.lightGray);
  g.fillRect(0,0,1000,1000);
  g.setColor(Color.white);
  g.fillRect(0,380,1000,150);
  g.setColor(Color.lightGray);
  g.fillRect(0,530,1000,470);
  dO.drawPineTree(700,200,150);
  dO.drawPoplarTree(400,50,150);
  dO.drawPoplarTree(440,100,250);
  dO.drawHouse(150,150,200);
  g.setColor(c);
  dO.drawCar(x,y,100,c);
  delay(20000000);
  changePosition(x,y);
}
```

```
public static void main(String[] args){
    ImportDraw iD = new ImportDraw();
}
}
```

Fig 11.4 A Simple Animation Example

Fig 11.5 The Output of
ImportDraw.java

The class DrawObjects, defined in Fig 11.2 is instantiated in this new Java class. Both classes use the symbol g for the instantiation of the Graphics class in their paint() methods. These must be set equal. This is done by the first instruction of the method public void paint(Graphics g) i.e.

dO.g = g;

The process of drawing must also be slowed down to human speed by use of the method void delay(long time). The car is driving along a white road, so, after showing the car for a short time, we must redraw the road over the top of the car's position and then we can redraw the car in its new position. In order to make it slightly more realistic, we have also incorporated some vertical as well as horizontal movement.

Java Graphics Performance Issues

The examples and exercises shown here allow for only one speed of operation. Even if we had multiple graphical objects changing their positions, they would all need to do so at the same speed, which would be a limitation on animation design. The solution to this problem is solved by 'multithreading' of graphical objects so that each object can move independently using small semi-autonomous programs–'threads' – within a single class.(See Chapter 15).

Serious real-world computer graphics are not easy to do effectively on a PC because of the nature of the machine and the Windows operating system. The PC is a general-purpose machine, designed to do, very effectively, a wide range of tasks from word processing to emailing, to database management, to Internet browsing and to a million other applications. Games programming machines with high speed graphics are relieved of most of these responsibilities so that the processor power can be dedicated to graphics animation only. For real-world computer animation, graphics which give the illusion of three-dimenionality must have a very high speed array- and floating-point trigonometric processing capacity.

Another limitation of performance using Java is that Java `.class` files are interpreted in real time. The Java Virtual Machine (JVM) must translate the byte code instructions to the computer's native machine code. This is a relatively slow process. compared with running executable files in **.exe** format directly.

Third party software utilities do exist to convert the `.class` files to **.exe** files. Such a utility would be used if one were to deploy software which had been originally written in Java since not every potential user has the JVM installed.

Java Quick and Easy

Chapter 11 Exercises

1. Write a program which places colored filled rectangles of size (50x50) on the csreen. The first rectangle has its top left-hand corner at point (100,100). Successive rectangles are displayed at points separated by 50 pixels along the horizontal line. As a rectangle is shown, its predecessor disappears. When the top LH of a rectangle corner reaches x = 1000, the next rectangle is shown on the row beneath i.e. with its top LH corner at (100,150). The rectangles go along the rows and progress down the screen until the row x position is at (100,1000). Then the program starts all over again until the window is closed.

2, Write a Java program to draw concentric disks of random colors. The disks begin with radius 300 pixels on the screen and reduce in radius by 10 pixels until the innermost circle has a radius of 20 pixels only. Then the program reverses itself and starts drawing increasingly larger disks until the radius is once again 300 pixels when the process reverses itself again and so on.

3. Draw a road of the shape shown on a white screen. A blue square enters the road at A and moves along the road to exit at B. The outer square is of size 500 x 500, the co-ordinates of A are (100,200) and (100,250) : the co-ordinates of B are (600,300) and (600,350). The road is 50 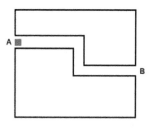 pixels wide, the blue square is of width 30 and the bend is at the midpoint of the outer square.

4. Write a Java program to simulate the rolling of a colored ball along a level path. The ball is formed by a black circle in which the four quadrants are colored alternately red and yellow.

5. Write a Java program to show your name on the screen in some large font. The name is gradually revealed as if a curtain is being pulled away from left to right.

6. Use the class `DrawObjects.java` defined in Fig 11.3 above to write a program which shows a red car in the middle of the screen. It has a small vertical 'wobble'. Meanwhile, a background with two trees moves past it from right to left. After some time the two trees come past again thus giving the impression of continuous motion.

7. Write a program which shows a simple ball bouncing between the two vertical walls of length 500 pixels at x = 100 and x = 1100. The ball leaves one wall and hits the opposite wall at some random point on it. The ball then returns to some random point on the first wall and so on until the program window is closed.

8. Draw a stylized airplane as shown. The airplane's wingspan and length are both 50 pixels in length. The airplane describes a circle on the screen with center at (500,500) and radius 400.

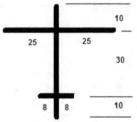

9. Write a program to imitate the passage of the seconds hand on a clock, i.e. a line sweeps out 6 degrees every second. Use the `Math` class library to work out the position of the ends of the 'hand'.

10. Write a program showing a simple 'matchstick' man who walks across the screen from left to write. His arms should move in synchronicity with his legs.

Chapter 12   Applets

So far, in this book, we have treated Java as a programming language for the development of regular PC-based applications. In fact, the language can be used for development in many diverse application areas from embedded firmware programs to large-scale commercial and industrial systems. The Java class libraries consist of reliable methods whose inner workings are guaranteed to be 100% reliable. The methods consist of small chunks of code invisible to the applications programmer and therefore immune to their arbitrary modifications.

Software reliability is particularly important if we are to use software to run our society. And not just the administration - computer programs are used in many life-critical areas - medicine, food and water supply, energy, transportation etc. Previous generations of programming languages were mostly procedural i.e. they required careful sequential programming. Since the programmer was usually responsible for the sequence and fine detail of the code, there were many opportunities for error. Mistakes were frequent with, sometimes, serious consequences. There is no doubt that the object-oriented 'paradigm', as it is called, has resulted in safer, more reliable code, a vital consideration if you are programming, say, an air traffic control system.

Another factor in the need for programming languages which are both safe and programmer-proof is that software systems have been growing in size exponentially since the dawn of the computer age. Moore's Law, that available computer power doubles about every eighteen months, is still as true today as when it was first formulated in 1968. Today's big systems may have hundreds millions of lines of code. As well as being reliable, that code needs to be easily maintained. Java does not guarantee absolute safety - there is still the human element - but its construction methodology and the copious built-in safety restraints make it more dependable than most of its rivals.

Java Quick and Easy

When Java was first invented, in the early 1990's, it was thought that its main use would be as an Internet language. Its birth more or less coincided exactly with the invention of the World Wide Web. Consequently, it was felt then that its main use would be in the creation of byte code programs could be transmitted over the Internet to new hosts where they could be run in the Java Virtual Machine of the receiving machine.

These small programs, embedded inside web pages for Internet transmission are called `applet`'s, to be run when the web page is opened at its destination. Textbooks about Java from that period concentrate on the `applet` as the principal product of Java software development.

Applets, though, bring with them a serious security problem. A malicious hacker might embed an insecure `applet` inside a web page before broadcasting that page far and wide. If there were no security precautions in place, a seemingly harmless page might contain an `applet` which could look at, or modify, files on the host computer.

To get over this problem, the original creators of Java, Sun Microsystems Inc, came up with the idea of a 'sandbox' – a protected area in the host machine's memory within which the `applet` could run safely. The Java Virtual Machine resided there together with the code and other resources included with the downloaded `applet`. The limits of the sandbox would be secured by a process of checking the `applet`'s byte code instruction when it is converted into the host machine native code to ensure that it did not address a host machine memory address outside the sandbox. The presence of such an instruction would cause the whole `applet` to be rejected.

As an added safety precaution, the designers of Java deliberately excluded pointer types from the Java language set. Pointers had been a feature of most third generation languages such as Pascal, Modula-2 and C++ where they are especially useful in the programming of dynamic data structures such as linked lists, stacks and queues.

Pointers are data types which contain, not data to be used directly, but addresses of other memory locations.

The insecurity of languages which have the pointer type is obvious if one considers that pointers can point to other pointers which can point to other pointers and so on. An ingenious malicious programmer could use programs to take the code outside the sandbox and into the host file system.

Better, thought the original Java language designers, not to have pointers at all. Java still has dynamic data structures like stacks and queues but they are safely encapsulated inside safe class libraries.

In a security conscious world, `applet`'s have now come to be regarded as too risky to be considered an important feature of the language, even though Java has gone from strength to strength in its range of applicability. The fundamental insecurity of the `applet` means that they are less important features of the language than the original designers of Java expected them to be.

Here is a very simple example, the `applet` equivalent of the traditional 'Hello World' program. There is no `main()` method as there would be in a regular application. The imported `Applet` class uses, instead, two `void` methods, `paint(Graphics g)` and `init()`. The first of these is standard `paint(Graphics g)` method of the `AWT` class as used in previous chapters. The second is, in effect, the constructor which starts the `applet` in the host machine and as for default constructors in regular Java applications, if the constructor is not needed, then it need not be defined.

Once the `applet` is written, then it is compiled to a `.class` file using **javac.exe** in the normal way. Applets do not need a separate `WindowAdapter` since window control is a function of the browser.

```
import java.awt.*;
import java.applet.*;
/*
<applet code = "FirstApplet" width = "840" height = "840">
</applet>
*/
```

```
public class FirstApplet extends Applet {
  Font f = new ont("Verdana",Font.BOLD|Font.ITALIC,48);
  public void paint(Graphics g){
    g.setFont(f);
    g.setColor(Color.red);
    g.drawString("First applet",50,100);
  }
}
```

Fig 12.1 The First Applet

There are two ways to test and run an applet like this. The first is to use a Java utility called **appletviewer.exe** which lies alongside **javac.exe** and **java.exe** in the *Program Files/Java/.../bin/* directory. To run your trial `applet` using **appletviewer** the comment

```
/*
<applet code = "FirstApplet" width = "400" height = "400">
</applet>
*/
```

must be included after the `import` statements and before the class declaration. Type the following instruction from the directory where you keep all your Java files.

```
>appletviewer FirstApplet.java
```

The second way is to write a HTML sript enclosing your applet and view it in your browser.

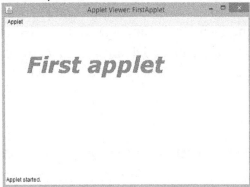

Fig 12.2
`FirstApplet.java`
as seen in appletviewer

The HTML script to run an `applet` looks something like

```
<html>
<head></head>
<body>
<applet code = "FirstApplet.class"
                      width = "400" height = "400">
</applet>
</body>
</html>
```

Fig 12.3 The HTML Page to Run `FirstApplet.class`

If you do decide to use your applet inside HTML to be read by a browser, then running the script of Fig 12.3 will not work immediately. Depending on which browser and operating system you are using, you will be prompted before the applet will be accepted.

Java Applet Security

When Java `applet`'s were first thought of, no one cared too much about computer security, or at least they worried about it less than we do now. Applets, unless they are carefully controlled, can act like Trojan horses, by importing viruses into the host machine.

However, we still need to be able to send harmless `applet`'s over a network. Each type of browser handles the problem differently. If your browser is Mozilla Firefox, for example, then you will be allowed to run the `applet` after a warning and a prompt. If your browser is Internet Explorer, which we are using here, then you will need to reset the Java security settings on the Java Control Panel (JCP) before you can run the web page containing your `applet`.

To change the security settings, first find the JCP and open it. In Windows 7 for example, the easiest way to reach it is to type 'Java Control Panel' in the textbox at the foot of the main program menu.

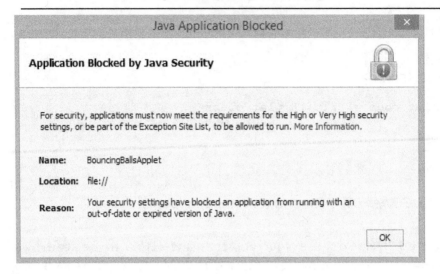

Fig 12.4 The applet is blocked

Fig 12.5 The Java Control Panel

You can also reach the Java Control Panel by running **javacpl.exe** which is in the *C:/Program Files/Java/../bin/* subdirectory. Then click on the 'Security' tab. In older versions of Java, a slider appears which indicates the security level set for incoming web software.

To run your `applet`, you must move the slider to its lowest, 'Medium', position. Later Java versions running under Windows 8 no longer have the 'Medium' security setting, just 'High' and 'Very High' radio buttons.

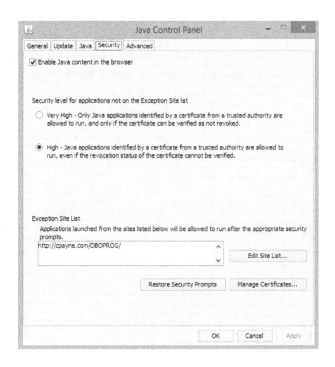

Fig 12.6 Setting the Security Level (Windows 8)

Once the security level has been set, you still cannot run your `applet` without a prompt appearing in a dialog box in front of the `applet` screen. Click on 'Run' and the `applet` output will displayed in the top left hand corner of the screen. The final output will be similar to the output from **appletviewer** as shown in Fig 12.2.

Those `applet`'s with a valid security certificate are automatically let through without the user needing to adjust the security level every time but it is still possible to run uncertificated applets from reliable senders by listing the site of its origin as a trusted site in the 'Exception Site List' `TextArea` box.

If you are developing your own applets online, it is a good idea to add your own site to the Exception Site List of trusted sites rather than re-setting the security level every time. In Windows 7 or higher you simply enter the site URL in the `TextArea` box beneath the "Security Level' control.

Be sure to remember to return the security settings back after you have tested your `applet`, since you will still be open to incoming messages .

The first time you download the `applet` via Internet Explorer from a trusted site on your list, you will get the following prompt.

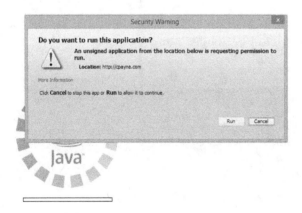

*Fig 12.7 Warning Box for First Download of a Page
from the Exception Site List.*

Thereafter, repeated downloads of the same page and applet will be displayed following the famous Java logo - the coffee cup.

Other browsers have a slightly different way of doing things. Whichever browser you use, the main principle - safety first - remains the same. Applets are an ideal way of passing on malicious viruses hidden in the byte code.

Java Applet Appearance

If I were developing an applet program for use on my own machine, I could use any font for `Label`'s `TextField`'s etc. But if I were to send this applet out on to the World Wide Web, I would need to use a commonly available font like Times New Roman or Verdana because not everyone has the full range of fonts. The browser at the destination will do its best by replacing a font it does not have with one of its own.

Absolute co-ordinates for graphics objects only make sense if you can be sure that the source and destination computers have exactly the same screen size. If this may not be the case then you will have to give up absolute positioning in favour of relative graphics object position via a `LayoutManager`. (See Chapter 13)

The Bouncing Balls Applet

The second `applet` example is `BouncingBalls.java`, a program which displays 10 colored disks. The balls, of randomly chosen size and color, move about the screen, bouncing off the sides of the screen.

```
import java.awt.*;
import java.awt.event.*;
import java.applet.*;
/*
<applet code =   "BouncingBallsApplet"
                 width = "800" height = "800">
</applet>
*/
public class BouncingBallsApplet extends Applet {
   Button b1;
   int numberBalls = 10;
   long shortTime;
```

```java
Color[] col;
int[] x,y,incX,incY,clearance,size;
public void init(){
  col = new Color[numberBalls];
  x = new int[numberBalls];
  y = new int[numberBalls];
  incX = new int[numberBalls];
  incY = new int[numberBalls];
  size = new int[numberBalls];
  clearance = new int[numberBalls];
  setBackground(Color.white);
  setLayout(null);
  setVisible(true);
  initializeIncXY();
  initializeColors();
  initializeSizes();
  setClearances();
  initializeXY();
  shortTime = calculateShortTime();
}
public long calculateShortTime(){
  return (3000000 - 20000*numberBalls);
}
public void initializeXY(){
  for (int i = 0; i < numberBalls; i++){
    x[i] = (int) Math.round(800*Math.random());
    y[i] = (int) Math.round(800*Math.random());
    while ((x[i] < 10) || (x[i] > clearance[i])){
      x[i] = (int) Math.round(800*Math.random());
    }
    while ((y[i] < 25) || (y[i] > clearance[i])){
      y[i] = (int) Math.round(800*Math.random());
    }
  }
}
 public void initializeIncXY(){
  for (int i = 0; i < numberBalls; i++){
    if (i%2 == 0){
      incX[i] = 1;
    }
    else
    {
      incX[i] = -1;
    }
      if ((i%3 == 0) || (i%5 == 0)){
      incY[i] = 1;
```

```
      }
      else
      {
        incY[i] = -1;
      }
    }
  }
  public void setClearances(){
    for (int i = 0; i < numberBalls; i++){
      clearance[i] = 800 - (size[i]/2);
    }
  }
  public void initializeColors(){
    int colorValue;
    Color c = Color.white;
    for (int i = 0; i < numberBalls; i++){
      colorValue = (int) Math.round(12*Math.random());
      switch(colorValue){
        case(0): c = Color.magenta; break;
        case(1): c = Color.black; break;
        case(2): c = Color.blue; break;
        case(3): c = Color.cyan; break;
        case(4): c = Color.darkGray; break;
        case(5): c = Color.gray; break;
        case(6): c = Color.green; break;
        case(7): c = Color.lightGray; break;
        case(8): c = Color.magenta; break;
        case(9): c = Color.orange; break;
        case(10): c = Color.pink; break;
        case(11): c = Color.red; break;
        case(12): c = Color.yellow;
      }
      col[i] = c;
    }
  }
  public void initializeSizes(){
    for (int i = 0; i < numberBalls; i++){
      size[i] = (int) Math.round(40*Math.random())+20;
    }
  }
  public void delay(long time){
    for (long i = 0; i < time; i++){}
  }
  public void changeXY(){
    for (int i = 0; i < numberBalls; i++){
      x[i] = x[i] + incX[i];
```

```
      y[i] = y[i] + incY[i];
      if ((x[i] == 10) || (x[i] == clearance[i])){
        incX[i] = -incX[i];
      }
      if ((y[i] == 25) || (y[i] == clearance[i])){
        incY[i] = -incY[i];
      }
    }
    repaint();
  }
  public void paint(Graphics g){
    g.setColor(Color.black);
    g.drawRect(10,25,805,795);
    for (int i = 0; i < numberBalls; i++){
      g.setColor(col[i]);
      g.fillOval(x[i],y[i],size[i],size[i]);
    }
    delay(shortTime);
    for (int i = 0; i < numberBalls; i++){
      g.setColor(Color.white);
      g.fillOval(x[i],y[i],size[i],size[i]);
    }
    delay(shortTime);
    changeXY();
  }
}
```

Fig 12.8 `BouncingBallsApplet.java`

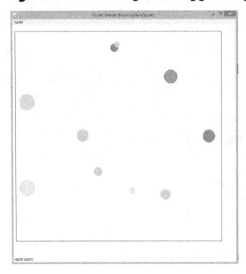

Fig 12.9 Output of
`BouncingBallsApplet.java`

<table>
<tr><th colspan="3">Comparison of Application and Applet Development</th></tr>
<tr><td></td><td>Application</td><td>Applet</td></tr>
<tr><td>import</td><td>-</td><td>import java.applet.*;</td></tr>
<tr><td>constructor</td><td>public ThisClass(){.....}</td><td>public void init(){.....}</td></tr>
<tr><td>class declaration</td><td>public class ThisClass extends Frame</td><td>public class ThisClass extends Applet</td></tr>
<tr><td>compilation</td><td>compile with javac.exe</td><td>compile with javac.exe</td></tr>
<tr><td>execution</td><td>java.exe
Add a main() method to run :
public static void main(String[] args){
ThisClass tC = new ThisClass();
}</td><td>appletviewer.exe or
.HTML script with browser</td></tr>
</table>

Chapter 12 Exercises

1. Write an `applet` which will show the French flag – vertical rectangular bands of `blue`, `white` and `red`, attached to a `black` flagstaff.

2. Write an `applet` which will display an image of size 100 x 100 in the center of the `applet` `Frame`. Add a line of description beneath the image.

3. Write and test a Java `applet` which will show a checkerboard of alternate `white` and `black` squares of size (40x40) in a 8x8 grid.

4. Write an `applet` with three `TextField`'s labeled "First Name:", "Middle Initial:" and "Surname:". The data is extracted when the 'ENTER' key is pressed and the concatenated string "FirstName" + ' ' + "middle Initial" + ' ' + "Surname" is output as a `Label`.

5. Create an `applet` with a `Label`, a `TextArea` and a `Button`. The `Label` is above the `TextArea` and has the message 'My Java Blog!!'. The

`Button` causes the text in the `TextArea` to be cleared just as if it had been uploaded to a server somewhere.

6. Convert the program from Question 5 into a regular Java application.

7. Write an `applet` in a frame of size 800 x 800 which will show the word 'JAVA! ' in the centre of the top line in Arial bold font size 12. Each time you click the mouse, this word is erased and written in the center of a line 16 pixels lower.

8. Develop the program in Question 2 and write an `applet` which will draw a square made up of an 8 x 8 grid of squares of size (40x40). In the center of each square is a smaller square as shown. Every row and column in the grid must contain eight different 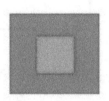 colors in which both the smaller and larger squares are different colors. No color, either of the larger or the smaller square, must appear more than once in each row and column.

9. Write an `applet` to display a stoplight with three colored lights – **39** red, yellow and green. the lights go on and off according to the sequence `red(50)`, `red + yellow(10)`, `green(60)`, `yellow(10)` and back to `red`. The times of this sequence are shown in parentheses. As a light is switched on, a counter starts ticking off the seconds.

10. Write an `applet` to simulate the rolling of a colored ball of diameter 100 pixels, down a 45° slope. The ball outline is a black circle of width 5 pixels. It has six equally–sized sectors colored blue, red and yellow. The ball moves increasingly quickly as it descends.

Chapter 13   LayoutManager's

LayoutManager's are needed when the target screen size is not known, such as e.g. when an `applet` is intended to be seen by someone at the other end of an Internet connection. The viewer may not have a screen of the same dimensions or screen resolution as the programmer of the applet, so all the `AWT` components and `Graphics` elements will not appear as the program designer wants you to see them.

As `applet`'s have lost their appeal because of security concerns, so the `LayoutManager` class is no longer quite so important when developing conventional Java applications. However, Java is used extensively in the development of so-called 'apps' for modern tablet devices.

Program development on tablets, SmartPhones and similar devices is Internet-based and many of them use Java graphics. These devices come in a wide variety of sizes and screen resolutions which makes the use of fixed co-ordinates for screen objects impossible. In that sort of small computer, a `LayoutManager` is essential. The operating system takes care of the actual physical locations of the screen objects when the app is downloaded at its destination.

Java provides a `LayoutManager` superclass for use in `applet` design. `FlowLayout` is the default and any program which imports the `AWT` will use it unless layout management has been in the class constructor:

```
setLayout(null);
```

FlowLayout

In a `FlowLayout`, screen objects are simply placed in the order in which they are added to the screen, starting from the top left hand corner. The constructors are :

```
FlowLayout()
FlowLayout(int how)
FlowLayout(int how,int horizontal,int vertical)
```

The first version is the basic form. In it, the objects are placed on screen as they appear, with 5 pixels horizontal spacing. If there is not enough room on the line for a new object, it is put on the next line with a vertical 5-pixel spacing separator.

The how argument describes the alignment method using three int constants, LEFT, CENTER and RIGHT. They describe how the flow objects are oriented within their regions. The third constructor is used when the spacing of horizontal and vertical data objects needs to be defined.

Here is a simple example. A collection of random objects is placed on an applet screen. The flow is centered and we specify a 20-pixel separation. The two buttons are present just to make up the numbers - they do nothing.

```java
import java.awt.*;
import java.awt.event.*;
import java.applet.*;
/*
<applet code = "FlowLayoutDemo" width = "250"
                                height = "200">
</applet>
*/
public class FlowLayoutDemo extends Applet{
  String s;
  Checkbox larry, curly, moe;
  Label l1, l2;
  Button b1,b2;
  TextField t1;
  public void init(){
    setLayout(new FlowLayout(FlowLayout.CENTER,20,20));
    setBackground(Color.yellow);
    setForeground(Color.blue);
    l1 = new Label("A FlowLayout Demo");
    add(l1);
    larry = new Checkbox("Larry Stooge");
    curly = new Checkbox("Curly Stooge",null,true);
    moe   = new Checkbox("Moe Stooge");
```

```
    add(larry);
    add(curly);
    add(moe);
    ItemListener listener = new MyItemListener();
    larry.addItemListener(listener);
    curly.addItemListener(listener);
    moe.addItemListener(listener);
    b1 = new Button("Not working!");
    b2 = new Button("Nor me! I'm just for show!");
    add(b1);
    add(b2);
    l2 = new Label("And the winning Stooge is...!");
    add(l2);
    t1 = new TextField();
    add(t1);
  }
  public void paint(Graphics g){
    s = "Larry "+ larry.getState()+ " Curly "+
        curly.getState()+ " Moe "+ moe.getState();
    t1.setText(s);
  }
  private class MyItemListener implements ItemListener{
    public void itemStateChanged(ItemEvent iE){
      repaint();
    }
  }
}
```

Fig 13.1 The `FlowLayoutDemo.java` *Program*

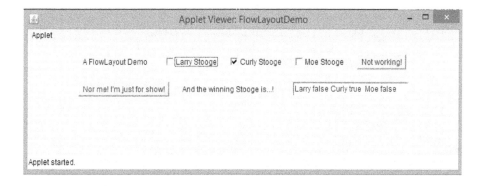

Fig 13.2 The Output of `FlowLayoutDemo.java`

BorderLayout

The `BorderLayout` class allows the programmer to put graphical items in five symmetrical screen positions and it provides the five constants called NORTH, EAST, SOUTH, WEST and CENTER to do so. These positions are defined when the item is added to the screen. The width of the positions is set at run time. Entering an object or text etc.to a position will cause the position to adjust its size to accommodate it.

```java
import java.awt.*;
import java.applet.*;
/*
<applet code = "BorderLayoutDemo" width = "400"
                                  height = "400">
 </applet>
*/
public class BorderLayoutDemo extends Applet{
   String s = "Now is the winter of our discontent";
   Font f = new Font("Verdana", Font.BOLD,18);
   Button bSouth;
   TextArea tA;
   Label lN,lW,lE;
   BorderLayout bL;
   public void init(){
      setLayout(new BorderLayout());
      setBackground(Color.lightGray);
      setForeground(Color.black);
      setFont(f);
      lN = new Label("The Border Layout Demo!" +
                     "This is NORTH",Label.CENTER);
      lW = new Label("WEST");
      lE = new Label("ËAST");
      bSouth = new Button("SOUTH is at the bottom!");
      add(lN,bL.NORTH);
      add(lW,bL.WEST);
      add(lE,bL.EAST);
      add(bSouth,bL.SOUTH); // add awt Labels
      tA = new TextArea(s);
      add(tA,bL.CENTER);
   }
}
```

Fig 13.3 Program `BorderLayoutDemo.java`

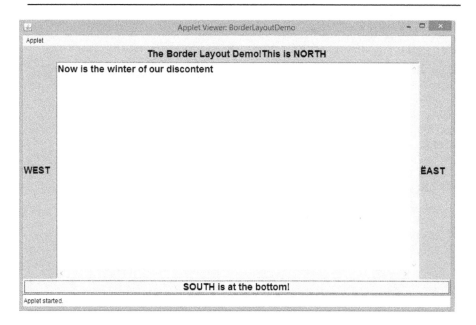

Fig 13.4 The Output of `BorderLayout.java`

GridLayout

Grid layouts allow the programmer to contain screen objects inside a regular grid of rows and columns. The `GridLayout` class has three constructors

```
GridLayout();
GridLayout(int numberOfRows,int numberOfColumns);
GridLayout(int numberOfRows,int numberOfColumns,
                        int horizontal, int vertical);
```

The two `int` variables `horizontal` and `vertical` define the number of pixels of spacing between columns and rows respectively. If the constructor has no arguments then it appears as a single column. If either dimension `numberOfRows` or `numberOfColumns` is set to zero, then the other dimension is unlimited. Here is a simple example which fills a 5 x 6 grid with numbered buttons. Spacing of 5 pixels is inserted between rows and columns.

145

```
import java.awt.*;
import java.applet.*;
/*
<applet code = "GridLayoutDemo" width="400" height=400">
</applet>
*/
public class GridLayoutDemo extends Applet{
  int n, rows = 5, cols = 6;
  public void init(){
    GridLayout gL = new GridLayout(rows,cols,5,5);
    Font f = new Font("SansSerif",Font.BOLD,20);
    setFont(f);
    setLayout(gL);
    for (int r = 0; r< rows; r++){
      for (int c = 0; c < cols; c++){
        n = r*cols + c + 1;
        add(new Button(Integer.toString(n)));
      }
    }
  }
}
```

Fig 13.5 A Program to Demonstrate GridLayout

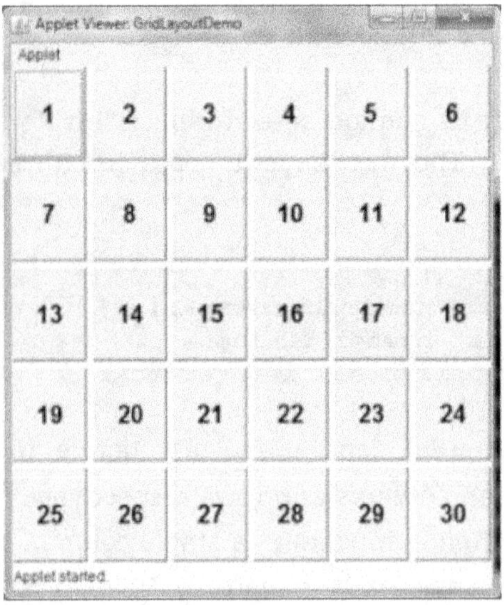

Fig 13.6 Output of GridLayoutDemo.java

This version of `GridLayoutDemo.java` has buttons which go to the very edge of the `applet`. To set the spacing away from the edges, the `LayoutManager` superclass uses the class

```
Insets(int top, int left, int bottom, int right);
```

The `getInsets()` method of `Insets` can be overridden to change the spacing to 15 pixels all round as in the following program.

```java
import java.awt.*;
import java.applet.*;
/*
<applet code = "GridLayoutDemoWithInsets"
                    width = "400" height = "400">
</applet>
*/
public class GridLayoutDemoWithInsets extends Applet{
  int n,rows = 5, cols = 6;
  public void init(){
    setBackground(Color.yellow);
    GridLayout gL = new GridLayout(rows,cols,5,5);
    Font f = new Font("SansSerif",Font.BOLD,20);
    setFont(f);
    setLayout(gL);
    for (int r = 0; r< rows; r++){
      for (int c = 0; c < cols; c++){
        n = r*cols + c + 1;
        add(new Button(Integer.toString(n)));
      }
    }
  }
  public Insets getInsets(){
    return new Insets(15,15,15,15);
  }
}
```

Fig 13.7 `GridLayoutWithInsets.java`

Fig 13.8 Output of `GridLayoutWithInsets.java`

If the constructor

```
GridLayout(int numberOfRows,int numberOfColumns,
                    int horizontal, int vertical);
```

has `numberOfRows` = 0, then the number of columns is unlimited.

Likewise, if `numberOfColumns` = 0, the number of rows can be made any value.Program 13.9 shows how to use this facility by defining the number of columns = 10, numbered 0..9.

```
import java.awt.*;
import java.applet.*;
/*
<applet code = "GridLayoutDemoUnlimitedColumns"
                width = "400" height = "100">
</applet>
*/

public class GridLayoutDemoUnlimitedColumns
                                extends Applet{
    int n;
    int cols = 10;  // This value is set
```

```
public void init(){
  setBackground(Color.yellow);
  GridLayout gL = new GridLayout(0,cols,5,5);
  Font f = new Font("SansSerif",Font.BOLD,20);
  setFont(f);
  setLayout(gL);
  for (int c = 0; c < cols; c++){
    add(new Button(Integer.toString(c)));
  }
}
```

Fig 13.9 Unlimited Columns in a Grid

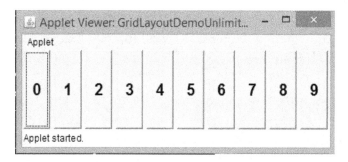

Fig 13.10 The Output of `GridLayoutDemoUnlimitedColumns.java`

Chapter 13 Exercises

1. Write and test a Java `applet` which will define a series of five `Label`'s called 'One', 'Two', 'Three', 'Four', 'Five' in a `FlowLayout` pattern in your `applet`. Test the `applet` in `appletviewer` and in a webpage on your local machine.

2. Convert the program in Question 1 to a regular Java application.

3. Write a Java `applet` to show three `TextField`'s and a `Button` in a `FlowLayout`. When the `Button` is pressed, the `applet` shows the contents of the three `TextField`'s as a concatenated `String` using the `Graphics.drawString()` method.

4. Modify your program in Question 3 so that the output of the concatenated `String` is to a `Label` instead of by the `Graphics.drawString()` method.

5. Write and test a Java `applet` which will place the five `Label`'s from Question 1 above in a `BorderLayout` displayed clockwise with `Label` 'Five' in the center.

6. Write and test a Java `applet` with four `Button`'s in the `NORTH`, `EAST`, `SOUTH` and `WEST` positions of a `BorderLayout`. The `CENTER` contains a centralized `TextField`. When a `Button` is pressed, the `TextField` displays the position of the `Button` press.

7. Write a Java `applet` with a `BorderLayout`. The three of the four outer regions (`NORTH`, `EAST`, `WEST`) have 20 character `TextField`'s. `SOUTH` has a `Button` which, when pressed, transfers the concatenated contents of the `TextField`'s to a `Label` in the `CENTER` of the applet.

8. Write and test a Java `applet` which will show a checkerboard of alternate `white` and `black` squares in a 8x8 grid.

9. Write an applet with a 9x3 `GridLayout`. Twenty six of the grid positions conain `Button`'s labelled 'A' to 'Z' . The twenty seventh position holds a `TextField` which records the letter of the `Button` which has been pressed.

10. Write a Java `applet` displaying a 4 x 4 `GridLayout` with a 10 pixel inset over a blue background. Each cell of the grid is a different random color.

Chapter 14 The Swing Classes

One solution to the problem of defining graphical screens which will look the same whatever the resolution and size of the target machine's screen and still be consistent with the 'write once run anywhere' Java philosophy is provided by Swing.

The classes and methods of the AWT are designed so that the translated byte code to run, for example, on a PC, must be translated into Intel™ native code before it becomes executable. So the form of the Java Virtual Machine will need to be rewritten for every different type of machine it is going to be run on. For graphics, as we have seen, this is particularly troublesome because, even if the processor instruction set were to be the same on two different machines, they may still have quite different screen sizes and different pixel densities.

The Swing classes duplicate and enhace the Windows components classes found in the AWT. This may seem redundant, but it does make perfect sense because the Swing classes are written in Java itself. Thus the same Swing components can be ported to any machine platform which contains a JVM without the need for different byte code translation versions of the Windows components.

Many program designers use only the Swing classes for Windows-type programming and leave the basic AWT classes alone. There is no need to do that if you are only going to be programming on a PC. What is more, it is perfectly possible to use both in the same application by mix-'n'-matching as you wish. Howevre, the Swing classes do offer increased functionality over those of the AWT which do similar things.

The Swing objects discussed here are:

```
JFrame        JPanel        JApplet      JLabel
ImageIcon     JTextField    JButton      JCheckBox
JRadioButton  JComboBox     JTabbedPane.
```

They are imported from the package javax.swing. The JFrame, JPanel and JApplet classes are 'container' objects which are used

Java Quick and Easy

in similar manner to their `AWT` equivalents i.e to hold Windows components.

JApplet

The `JApplet` can be drawn in a `contentPane`, defined by the method

`Container getContentPane().`

The `contentPane` sits inside the `JApplet`. The method

`void add(component)`

is used to add components to the `contentPane` and hence to the `JApplet`. (See example 14.1 below)

JLabel

`JLabel` is the `Swing` equivalent of the `AWT` `Label` class with constructors :

```
JLabel(ImageIcon i);
JLabel(String s);
JLabel(String s, ImageIcon i, int align)
```

The `align` argument takes one of three `JLabel` `int` constants, `LEFT`, `RIGHT` or `CENTER` and describes the placing of a `JLabel` content within its defining `Container`.

`JLabel` adds label functionality by permitting the adding of images, or `ImageIcon`'s to it. This first example is the `Swing` equivalent of the "HelloWorld" type of program. It just displays a single `JLabel` in an applet. The image and the text are aligned according to the constant `align` – in this case it is `CENTER`'ed inside its `contentPane`. If the image file is not present, the program runs, but simply omits the image.

152

```
import java.awt.*;
import javax.swing.*;
/*
<applet code="JLabelDemo" width = "250" height = "250">
</applet>
*/
public class JLabelDemo extends JApplet{
  public void init() {
    Container contentPane = getContentPane();
            // Holds the content in a JApplet
    Font f = new Font("SansSerif",Font.BOLD,24);
    ImageIcon i = new ImageIcon("TowerBridgeLondon.jpg");
    contentPane.setBackground(Color.pink);
    JLabel jL = new JLabel("Tower Bridge London",i,
                        JLabel.CENTER);
    jL.setFont(f);
    jL.setForeground(Color.blue);
    contentPane.add(jL);
  }
}
```

Fig 14.1 `JLabelDemo.java`

The `ImageIcon` is a *JPG* image file . One could use a `try..catch` to test for the presence of the file in the current directory.

The program `JLabelDemo.java` also imports `java.awt` without which it would not have access to the access to the `Container`, `Font` and `Color` classes.

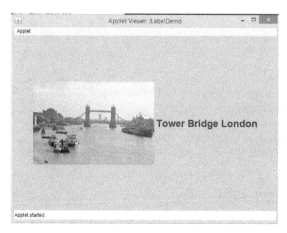

Fig 14.2 Output of `JLabelDemo.java`

ImageIcon

As we have seen in the last example, `Swing` allows for the attachment of Images of the class `ImageIcon`. The images themselves are defined by their filename/directory or their URL address and there is a constructor for each.

```
ImageIcon(String filename);
ImageIcon(URL url); - url is an image at the given web address
```

Methods for `ImageIcon` include:

```
int getIconHeight();
int getIconWidth()
void paintIcon(Component comp, Graphics g, int x, int y);
```

which paints the `ImageIcon` in a container object at location (x,y).

The `Swing` classes are not just for `applet`'s, they can be used in regular applications. The next program example is an application and the containing drawing area is `JFrame`, not a `contentPane`. To convert from an applet to an application, we can add `JFrame`, `setSize`, a possible `WindowListener`, `setVisible()` and a `main()` method to replace `init()`. In this example we also import the `Swing` components individually from `javax` as an alternative to using the *-notation.

```
import java.awt.*;
import java.awt.event.*;
import javax.swing.JFrame;
import javax.swing.ImageIcon;
import javax.swing.JLabel;
public class SwingImageDemo extends JFrame{
  public SwingImageDemo(){
    JLabel jL;
    ImageIcon iI;
    FlowLayout fL = new FlowLayout();
    setLayout(fL);
    setTitle("Using JLabel in an application");
```

```
    setSize(500,500);
    addWindowListener(new MyWindowAdapter());
    Font f = new Font("Verdana",Font.BOLD,28);
    iI = new ImageIcon("EnglishCountryHouse.jpg");
    jL = new JLabel("English Country House",iI,
                              JLabel.CENTER);
    jL.setFont(f);
    jL.setForeground(Color.blue);
    add(jL);
    setVisible(true);
  }
  public static void main(String[] args){
    SwingImageDemo sID = new SwingImageDemo();
  }
}
```

Fig 14.3 Using Swing Classes to Display an Image

Fig 14.4 The Output of SwingImageDemo.java

JTextField

The following JApplet shows how to define a JTextField, the Swing equivalent of the AWT class TextField. The text could be set or returned using the two methods :

```
JTextField.setText(String s);
```
and
```
String s = JTextField.getText();
```

Here is a simple example of using these methods with a JTextField object.

```
import java.awt.*;
import javax.swing.*;
import java.awt.event.*;
/*
<applet code = "JTextFieldExample" width = "300"
                                    height = "100">
</applet>
*/
public class JTextFieldExample extends JApplet{
  JLabel jL = new JLabel("");
  JTextField jTF = new JTextField(5);
  String s;
  public void init() {
    Container contentPane = getContentPane();
    Font f = new Font("Arial",Font.BOLD,24);
    FlowLayout fL = new FlowLayout();
    contentPane.setLayout(fL);
    jTF.setFont(f);
    jL.setFont(f);
    contentPane.add(jTF);
    contentPane.add(jL);
    jTF.addActionListener(new MyActionListener());
  }
  private class MyActionListener implements
                                  ActionListener{
    public void actionPerformed(ActionEvent aE){
      s = jTF.getText();
      jL.setText(s);
    }
  }
}
```

Fig 14.5 `JTextFieldExample.java`

Java Quick and Easy

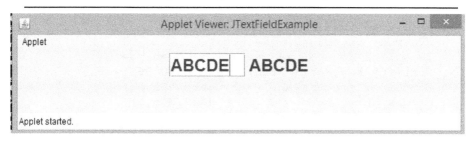

Fig 14.6 Output of `JTextFieldExample.java`

JButtons with Images

The extra functionality of `Swing` compared with the `AWT` is shown in the following `JApplet` example. The `AWT` Buttons only come in plain gray but we can add an `ImageIcon` to a `JButton` to enhance the appearance of a GUI. In the next program, each `JButton` in a group carries an image of a national flag. The `JTextFIeld` records the name of the country as its flag is clicked. The images can be in any standard image format. The flags of France, Japan, Sweden and Russia can be quickly drawn using any graphics software. The Stars and Stripes, the flag of the USA, is the output of the Exercise Chapter 7, No. 10. `JButtons` respond to the `ActionListener` interface commands and include a useful method

```
JButton.setActionCommand(String s);
```

which returns a `String` for display when the `JButton` is clicked.

```
import java.awt.*;
import java.awt.event.*;
import javax.swing.*;
/*
<applet code = "ButtonsWithImages"
                width = "250" height = "300">
</applet>
*/
public class ButtonsWithImages extends JApplet{
   JTextField jTF;
```

```
public void init() {
   JButton jB1,jB2,jB3,jB4,jB5;
   ImageIcon france,usa,japan,russia,sweden;
   Font f = new Font("Arial",Font.BOLD,36);
   Container contentPane = getContentPane();
   GridLayout gL = new GridLayout(2,3,5,5);
   contentPane.setLayout(gL);
   ActionListener listener = new MyActionListener();
   france = new ImageIcon("france.jpg");
   jB1 = new JButton(france);
   jB1.setActionCommand("France");
   jB1.addActionListener(listener);
   contentPane.add(jB1);
   usa = new ImageIcon("usa.jpg");
   jB2 = new JButton(usa);
   jB2.setActionCommand("USA");
   jB2.addActionListener(listener);
   contentPane.add(jB2);
   japan = new ImageIcon("japan.jpg");
   jB3 = new JButton(japan);
   jB3.setActionCommand("Japan");
   jB3.addActionListener(listener);
   contentPane.add(jB3);
   russia = new ImageIcon("russia.jpg");
   jB4 = new JButton(russia);
   jB4.setActionCommand("Russia");
   jB4.addActionListener(listener);
   contentPane.add(jB4);
   sweden = new ImageIcon("sweden.jpg");
   jB5 = new JButton(sweden);
   jB5.setActionCommand("Sweden");
   jB5.addActionListener(listener);
   contentPane.add(jB5);
   jTF = new JTextField(20);
   jTF.setFont(f);
   contentPane.add(jTF);
}
private class MyActionListener implements
                          ActionListener{
   public void actionPerformed(ActionEvent aE){
     jTF.setText("        " + aE.getActionCommand());
   }
}
}
```

Fig 14.7 Attaching Images to Buttons

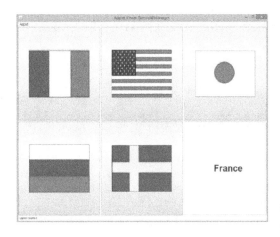

France

Fig 14.8 Attaching Images to Buttons – the Output

JCheckBox

The `JCheckBox` is much more versatile than its AWT equivalent. For example, we can add icons to the screen to indicate whether or not the cursor is on top of the icon, whether the icon's `JCheckBox` has been ticked or whether it is in its normal passive state.

JCheckBox constructors come in six variants i.e with or without a `String` identifier, with or without an `ImageIcon` attached and whether the box is checked or not. The `boolean state` is `true` when JCheckBox is ticked. The six `JCheckBox` constructors are:

```
JCheckBox(ImageIcon i);
JCheckBox(ImageIcon i, boolean state);
JCheckBox(String s);
JCheckBox(String s, boolean state);
JCheckBox(String s, ImageIcon i);
JCheckBox(String s, ImageIcon i, boolean state);
```

Here is a use of `JCheckBox`. As the mouse moves it signals if it is over one of the images. When this happens the `JCheckBox` image changes color and its label changes from 'Normal' to 'Rollover'.

159

If a `JCheckBox` is selected, a different Image appears, showing 'Selected' and a message appears in the `JTextField`. The `JCheckBox` names are 'Pepperoni', 'Cheese' and 'Plain'.

```java
import java.awt.*;
import java.awt.event.*;
import javax.swing.*;
public class SwingCheckBox extends JFrame{
  JTextField jTF;
  JCheckBox jCB;
  String s;
  public SwingCheckBox(){
    FlowLayout fL = new FlowLayout();
    setLayout(fL);
    setTitle("Using JCheckBox in an application");
    setSize(300,300);
    ItemListener listener = new MyItemListener();
    addWindowListener(new MyWindowAdapter());
    ImageIcon normal = new ImageIcon("NormalIcon.jpg");
    ImageIcon rollover = new
                        ImageIcon("RolloverIcon.jpg");
    ImageIcon selected = new
                        ImageIcon("SelectedIcon.jpg");
    JCheckBox cB1 = new JCheckBox("Pepperoni",normal);
    cB1.setRolloverIcon(rollover);
    cB1.setSelectedIcon(selected);
    cB1.addItemListener(listener);
    add(cB1);
    JCheckBox cB2 = new JCheckBox("Cheese",normal);
    cB2.setRolloverIcon(rollover);
    cB2.setSelectedIcon(selected);
    cB2.addItemListener(listener);
    add(cB2);
    JCheckBox cB3 = new JCheckBox("Plain",normal);
    cB3.setRolloverIcon(rollover);
    cB3.setSelectedIcon(selected);
    cB3.addItemListener(listener);
    add(cB3);
    jCB = new JCheckBox();
    jTF = new JTextField(14);
    add(jTF);
    setVisible(true);
  }
```

```
private class MyItemListener implements ItemListener{
  public void itemStateChanged(ItemEvent iE){
    jCB = (JCheckBox) iE.getItem();
    s = jCB.getText();
    jTF.setText(s);
  }
}
public static void main(String[] args){
  SwingCheckBox cB = new SwingCheckBox();
}
}
```

Fig 14.9 Using `JCheckBox`

The output is shown in Fig 14.10. The `JCheckBox` "Pepperoni" has been chosen and clicked. The mouse is currently above the "Cheese" image and the "Plain" selection is in its passive state.

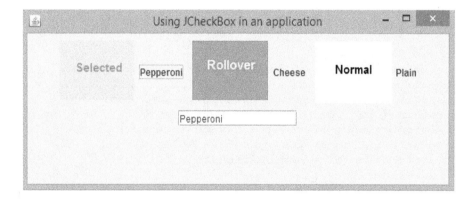

Fig 14.10 The Output of `SwingCheckBox.java`

JRadioButton

The class `JRadioButton` is like its `AWT` `Checkbox` equivalent. `JRadioButton`"s can also be grouped as in the following application. Each is added separately to the `JFrame` and a `JTextField` records which `JButton` has been chosen. As for `JCheckBox`, there are six

161

constructors – an `ImageIcon` and/or a `String` label can be attached alongside the `JRadioButton`.

The constructors of `JRadioButton` are :

```
JRadioButton(ImageIcon i);
JRadioButton(ImageIcon i, boolean state);
JRadioButton(String s);
JRadioButton(String s, boolean state);
JRadioButton(String s, ImageIcon i);
JRadioButton(String s,ImageIcon i,boolean state);
```

The `boolean` variable `state` indicates `true` if the `JRadioButton` is chosen.

```
import java.awt.*;
import java.awt.event.*;
import javax.swing.*;
public class SwingRadio extends JFrame{
  JTextField jTF;
  ButtonGroup bG;
  Font f = new Font("Arial",Font.BOLD,24);
  public SwingRadio(){
    FlowLayout fL = new FlowLayout();
    setLayout(fL);
    setTitle("Using JRadioButton in an application");
    setSize(300,300);
    ActionListener listener = new MyListener();
    addWindowListener(new MyWindowAdapter());
    JRadioButton b1 = new JRadioButton("Larry");
    b1.setFont(f);
    b1.addActionListener(listener);
    add(b1);
    JRadioButton b2 = new JRadioButton("Curly");
    b2.setFont(f);
    b2.addActionListener(listener);
    add(b2);
    JRadioButton b3 = new JRadioButton("Moe");
    b3.setFont(f);
    b3.addActionListener(listener);
    add(b3);
    bG = new ButtonGroup();
    bG.add(b1);
    bG.add(b2);
```

```
    bG.add(b3);
    jTF = new JTextField(20);
    jTF.setFont(f);
    add(jTF);
    setVisible(true);
  }
  private class MyListener implementsActionListener{
    public void actionPerformed(ActionEvent aE){
      jTF.setText(aE.getActionCommand());
    }
  }
  public static void main(String[] args){
    SwingRadio sR = new SwingRadio();
  }
}
```

Fig 14.11 SwingRadio.java – *Using* JRadioButton

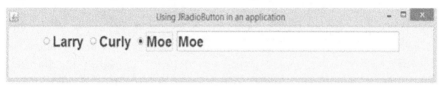

Fig 14.12 Output of SwingRadio.java

JComboBox

The JComboBox needs a small addition to its definition.. This is because the items it lists are not simple types. In fact a JComboBox can contain items of many different types – String, int, double *etc*. Simply to try to construct it from a constructor like

```
JComboBox jCB = new JComboBox()
```

in the usual way will result in a compiler error. This is because the type of the item inside the list, a primitive type or an object, is not specified.

The data type of the list items are said to be "raw" i.e. in need of further definition. A fairly late change to Java, some fifteen years after the language first made its debut, corrected this anomaly. The

Java Quick and Easy

JComboBox constructor uses a new notation – the "diamond" notation – to create a safe definition. The basic forms of the constructors are :

```
JComboBox<Object>();
JComboBox<Object>(Vector v);
```

where (Vector v) forms the list of items for selection. It can contain any primitive type or object defined in <Object>.

Items can also be added to the JComboBox dynamically using the method.

```
void addItem(Object oB);
```

The following application, SwingComboBox.java, shows how this notation works. The program creates a JComboBox and adds four items to it. When an item is selected, its related image is also shown. The class for the items is String, so we include "String" in diamond notation. Note also the use of the setIcon() method of JLabel inside the inner private class.

```java
import java.awt.*;
import java.awt.event.*;
import javax.swing.*;
public class SwingComboBox extends JFrame{
   JLabel jL;
   ImageIcon pepperoni,extracheese;
   ImageIcon plain,extracheeseandpepperoni;
   Font f;
   public SwingComboBox(){
     FlowLayout fL = new FlowLayout();
     setLayout(fL);
     setTitle("Using JComboBox in an application");
     setSize(500,500);
     f = new Font("Arial",Font.BOLD,24);
     ItemListener listener = new MyItemListener();
     addWindowListener(new MyWindowAdapter());
     JComboBox<String> jC = new JComboBox<String>();
     jC.setFont(f);
     jC.addItem("plain");
     jC.addItem("pepperoni");
     jC.addItem("extracheese");
```

```
        jC.addItem("extracheeseandpepperoni");
        jC.addItemListener(listener);
        add(jC);
        jL = new JLabel(new ImageIcon("plain.jpg"));
        jL.setFont(f);
        add(jL);
        setVisible(true);
    }
    private class MyItemListener implements
    ItemListener{
        public void itemStateChanged(ItemEvent iE){
            String s = (String) iE.getItem();
            jL.setIcon(new ImageIcon(s + ".jpg"));
        }
    }
    public static void main(String[] args){
        SwingComboBox sCB = new SwingComboBox();
    }
}
```

Fig 14.13 Using a `JComboBox` *in an Application.*

Fig 14.14 Output of `SwingComboBox.java`

JTabbed Pane

The `JTabbedPane` allows us to tab multiple options on different panes in the same `JFrame`. Each of the three panes in this program has a

165

different selection mechanism. Depending on the tab chosen, the selection will be via multiple `JButton`'s, `JCheckBox`'s or a `JComboBox`.

Each of these three `Swing` objects is attached to its own `JPanel` which is defined in a separate `private` inner class.

```java
import javax.swing.*;
import java.awt.*;
public class SwingTabbedPane extends JFrame{
  public SwingTabbedPane(){
    JTabbedPane jTP = new JTabbedPane();
    jTP.addTab("Pizzas", new PizzasPanel());
    jTP.addTab("Topping", new ToppingsPanel());
    jTP.addTab("Sizes", new SizesPanel());
    add(jTP);
    FlowLayout fL = new FlowLayout();
    setLayout(fL);
    setTitle("Using JTabbedPane in an application");
    setSize(500,500);
    setVisible(true);
  }
  private class PizzasPanel extends JPanel{
    public PizzasPanel(){
      JButton b1 = new JButton("Regular");
      JButton b2 = new JButton("Thin Crust");
      JButton b3 = new JButton("Thick Crust");
      JButton b4 = new JButton("Herb Dough");
      add(b1);
      add(b2);
      add(b3);
      add(b4);
    }
  }
  private class ToppingsPanel extends JPanel{
    public ToppingsPanel(){
      JCheckBox cB1 = new JCheckBox("Cheese");
      JCheckBox cB2 = new JCheckBox("Pepperoni");
      JCheckBox cB3 = new JCheckBox("Hawaiian");
      JCheckBox cB4 = new JCheckBox("Veggie");
      add(cB1);
      add(cB2);
      add(cB3);
      add(cB4);
    }
  }
```

```
private class SizesPanel extends JPanel{
  public SizesPanel(){
    JComboBox<String> coB = new JComboBox<String>();
    coB.addItem("4\"");
    coB.addItem("8\"");
    coB.addItem("10\"");
    coB.addItem("12\"");
    add(coB);
  }
}
public static void main(String[] args){
  SwingTabbedPane sTP = new SwingTabbedPane();
}
}
```

Fig 14.15 Using a `JTabbedPane`

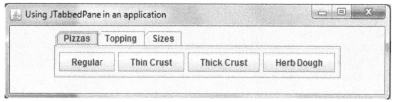

Fig 14.16i The Effect of pressing "Pizza" – four `JButton's`

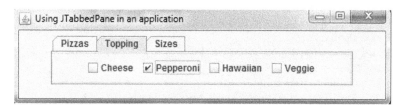

Fig 14.16ii The Effect of pressing "Topping" – four `JCheckBox"s`

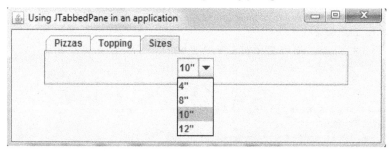

Fig 14.16iii The Effect of pressing "Sizes" – a `JComboBox`

Java Quick and Easy

Mixing AWT and Swing Controls

The `Swing` components offer better functionality compared with their AWT equivalents and are generally preferred in applications which only use the Windows objects. But `Swing` does not replace the `AWT` completely. For basic drawn graphics, the `AWT` must still be used, as must the `import java.awt.event.*`. It is perfectly acceptable to mix `Swing` and AWT components. The following example sends the output of a `JTextField` to a `Graphics.drawString()` when the input `String` terminates with a CRLF.

```
import java.awt.*;
import javax.swing.*;
import java.awt.event.*;
public class MixingSwingAndAWT extends JFrame{
  Font f = new Font("Arial",Font.BOLD,18);
  JTextField jTF;
  public MixingSwingAndAWT (){
    setLayout(null);
    setSize(400,400);
    setTitle("Mixing AWT and Swing");
    jTF = new JTextField(20);
    jTF.setFont(f);
    jTF.setBounds(20,20,200,40);
    add(jTF);
    setVisible(true);
    addWindowListener(new MyWindowAdapter());
    ActionListener listener = new MyActionListener();
    jTF.addActionListener(listener);
  }
  private class MyActionListener implements
      ActionListener{
    public void actionPerformed(ActionEvent aE){
      repaint();
    }
  }
  public void paint(Graphics g){
    g.setFont(f);
    g.drawString(jTF.getText(),200,200);
  }
  public static void main(String args[]){
```

```
    MixingSwingAndAWT jTFE = new MixingSwingAndAWT();
  }
}
```

Fig 14.17 Mixing Swing
and the AWT

Chapter 14 Exercises

1. Write and test a JApplet with a JLabel on the left of the screen bearing the message "I LOVE JAVA!!!!" in green on a yellow background.

2. Use the Swing components to write a JApplet containing a JButton with an image. When it is pressed, it will cause a JLabel to become visible.

3. Write a Swing JApplet with a JLabel and two JButton's. The two JButton's change the foreground and background colors of the JLabel at random.

4. Convert the program in Question 3 to a regular application.

5. Write an application with a JTextField. When the ENTER key is pressed the contents of the JTextField are displayed below it on a JLabel.

Java Quick and Easy

6. Write a `JApplet` with four `Swing` `JRadioButton`'s in a group. The `JButton`'s are labelled "Eeny", "Meany", "Miney", "Mo". The chosen `JButton` is displayed via a `JLabel`.

7. Write an application to show two `JComboBox`"s inside a `JFrame`. The first `JComboBox` has a label "Tablet size" and has items of type `int` with values 3, 5, 7, 10. The second `JComboBox` is titled "Screen type" and contains a list of `String`"s with values "VGA", EGA", "SVGA" and "XVGA". The choice of size and type is output to a `JTextField` which combines the `int` output of the first `JComboBox` and the `String` output of the second `JComboBox`. Enhance your screen with a downloaded clipart image of a computer monitor.

8. Write an application which will create a gallery of ten `ImageIcon`"s in a 5x2 `GridLayout`. Each `ImageIcon` will be positioned symmetrically inside the grid. Title the page using a `JLabel` with the legend "My Photo Gallery" in the centre of the screen.

9. Write an application using four `JCheckBox`"s with images showing Roman numerals "I", "II", "III" and "IV". The `JCheckBox`"s may be selected, rolled over or waiting. Indicate the status of each by an array of `JLabels` which is updated every time the state changes e.g.

I is selected
II is waiting
III is rolled over
IV is waiting

10. Write an application with a tabbed pane in a `JFrame`. Show two tabs labeled "Nationality" and "Sex". The first tab presents a `JCheckBox` group of two boxes labeled "Eligible" and "Not Eligible". The second tab also produces a `JCheckBox` group of two boxes labeled "Male" and "Female". The result of checking the boxes is returned to a `JLabel`.

Java Quick and Easy

Chapter 15   Multithreading

Modern computers multitask heavily to take advantage of their very high speed processors. This was not always the case. The first two generations of computers, now museum pieces, could only do one thing at a time. This was also the case with the first generation of microcomputers such as the MSDOS machines of the 1980's. In those far off days, a microcomputer would have to suspend its CPU until a slow operation such as the printing of a document had been completed. It was very inefficient.

Today"s machines can do many things seemingly simultaneously. One can be word processing, printing and downloading files all at the same time, while, in the background, the operating system is also taking care of the file housekeeping, reading the keyboard input and updating the screen. So computers "multitask" by constantly switching from one task to another to take advantage of the surplus capacity of the bus and the processor. This multitasking appears simultaneous to us, the human users, because we are by far the slowest part of an information system. In fact, most computers still process their commands sequentially.

Most operating systems perform multitasking by dividing their operations into "chunks" of program code called "processes". A process roughly approximates to a basic program unit, such as a window or a dialog box. A multitasking computer may have large numbers of these processes at any moment, all but one of them awaiting its turn to run.

Processes are large objects and consume considerable processor resources. A smaller way of multitasking is to use "threading", where different strands of program code can be executed in turn from within the same program and process. This "slimline" version of multitasking means that a number of "subprograms" or threads are controlled by the same program. It provides, for example, a better way of controlling multiple screen graphics operations for programming animations than the method we described in Chapter 11 where all our screen changes

171

have to take place at the same speed. Multithreading allows the various animation objects to move independently of each other.

The program `FirstThreadDemo.java` illustrates the use of a single `Thread` in a controlling program. The main parent `Thread` is created by the program"s `main()` method. All the program does is to invoke the `sleep` method of the main `Thread` to slow down the printing of the descending set of numbers. All `Thread`"s must have a `try..catch` control to catch exceptions which may be caused by unforeseen events e.g. if their sleep is interrupted.

```java
public class FirstThreadDemo{
  public static void main(String[] args){
    Thread t = Thread.currentThread();
          // the main() method is the current thread
    t.setName("First Thread Demo");
    System.out.println("  Java Quick and Easy " + t);
    try{
      for (int i = 10; i>0; i--){
        System.out.println("   " + i);
        t.sleep(2000);// sleeps for 2000 msec
      }
    }
    catch(InterruptedException iE){
      System.out.println("  Main thread interrupted");
    }
    System.out.println("  Program cycle finished");
  }
}
```

Fig 15.1 `FirstThreadDemo.java`

```
Java Quick and Easy Thread[First Thread Demo,5,main]
10
9
8
7
6
5
4
3
2
1

Program cycle finished
```

Fig 15.2 Output of `FirstThreadDemo.java`

Java Quick and Easy

`FirstThreadDemo.java` is not a very useful program. Its only purpose is to slow down the presentation of output values. More useful is the creation of child `Thread`"s which do something of their own. For this, we need to implement the interface `Runnable`, which allows for the transfer of control between different threads.

In the following example, `NewThreadDemo.java`, we move between the main `Thread` and a separate independent child `Thread`. This child `Thread` is called `NewThread.java` and its code is shown in Fig 15.3. It implements `Runnable` and it uses two important methods, `start()` and `run()` which define the entry point of the child `Thread`.

```
public class NewThread implements Runnable{
  Thread t;
  int visitor = 1;
  public NewThread(){
    t = new Thread();
    t.setName("Demo Thread   ");
    System.out.println("  Child thread   " + t);
    t.start();
  }
  public void run(){   // entry point for child thread
    try{
      System.out.println("  BBBBB       - in child thread"
                  + "Visit = " + visitor);
      visitor++;
      Thread.sleep(2000);
    }
    catch(InterruptedException iE){
      System.out.println("  Child thread interrupted");
    }
  }
}
```

Fig 15.3 `NewThread.java`

When `NewThread` is running, it will execute the line

```
    System.out.println
  ("BBBBB    - in child thread Visit = " + visitor);
```

before sleeping for 2000 milliseconds and returning control to its parent. We still have to define the parent, `NewThreadDemo.java`, which is shown in Fig 15.4.

```
public class NewThreadDemo {
  public static void main(String[] args){
    NewThread t1 = new NewThread();
    int counter = 5;
    while (counter > 0) {
      try{
        System.out.println
          ("AAAAA - main thread "+ "counter = " + counter);
        Thread.sleep(1000);
        t1.run();
      }
      catch(InterruptedException iE){
        System.out.println("Failed!!!");
      }
      counter--;
    }
    System.out.println("Main thread finished.");
  }
}
```

Fig 15.4 The Parent Thread, `NewThreadDemo.java`

The two classes could be compiled separately although the `Thread NewThread.class` is here defined inside its parent thread. The `main` method of the parent starts the child `Thread` via its `start()` method when the child constructor is executed. The parent `Thread` in Fig 15.4 simply sleeps for 1000 milliseconds and then passes control to its child, (Fig 15.3). The child then uses its method, `t1.run()` and a `String` of output is sent to the console after which the `Thread` goes back to sleep. The output is shown in Fig 15.5

The next example is an extension of the program `NewThreadDemo.java`. After the `main` method starts and instantiates the two child `Thread` classes, control of the program is passed from the `main()` method of `NewThreadsSecondDemo("AAAAA")` to `NewChildThreadB("BBBBB")`, and then to `NewChildThreadC("CCCCC")`, in a cycle.

```
Child thread   Thread[Demo Thread   ,5,main]

AAAAA - main thread counter = 5
BBBBB        - in child thread  Visit = 1

AAAAA - main thread counter = 4
BBBBB        - in child thread  Visit = 2

AAAAA - main thread counter = 3
BBBBB        - in child thread  Visit = 3

AAAAA - main thread counter = 2
BBBBB        - in child thread  Visit = 4

AAAAA - main thread counter = 1
BBBBB        - in child thread  Visit = 5

Main thread finished.
```

Fig 15.5. The Output of `NewThreadDemo.java`

As each child `Thread` sleeps, it passes the processor over to the next `Thread`. During this time, the main controlling `while` loop in `main()` is still running and the three phase cycle continues until the `while` logic control shows `false`. `NewThreadsSecondDemo.java` includes all the classes in one file although `NewChildThreadB` and `NewChildThreadC` are autonomous and could be compiled separately as `public` classes.

```
public class NewThreadsSecondDemo {
  public static void main(String[] args){
    NewChildThreadB tB = new NewChildThreadB();
    NewChildThreadC tC = new NewChildThreadC();
    int counter = 5;
    while (counter > 0) {
      try{
        System.out.println();
        System.out.println
        ("   AAAAA - main thread counter = " + counter);
        tB.run();
        tC.run();
        Thread.sleep(1000);
      }
      catch(InterruptedException iE){
        System.out.println
        ("   Main thread AAAAA " + "interrupted");
      }
      counter--;
```

```
    }
    System.out.println();
    System.out.println("  Main thread finished.");
  }
}
class NewChildThreadB implements Runnable{
  Thread t;
  int visit = 0;
  public NewChildThreadB(){
    t = new Thread();
    t.start();
  }
  public void run(){  // child thread entry point
    try{
      System.out.println("    BBB - first child thread " +
                      "Visit = " +  visit);
      visit++;
      Thread.sleep(1000);
    }
    catch(InterruptedException iE){
      System.out.println("  Child thread BBB nterrupted");
    }
  }
}
class NewChildThreadC implements Runnable{
  Thread t;
  int visit = 0;
  public NewChildThreadC(){
    t = new Thread();
    t.start();
  }
  public void run(){  // entry of second(child) thread
    try{
      System.out.println
      ("      C  - second child thread " +
                        "Visit = " + visit);
      visit++;
      Thread.sleep(1000);
    }
    catch(InterruptedException iE){
      System.out.println("Child thread C interrupted");
    }
  }
}
```

Fig 15.6 NewThreadsSecondDemo.java

```
AAAAA - main thread counter = 5
  BBB - first child thread Visit = 0
    C - second child thread Visit = 0

AAAAA - main thread counter = 4
  BBB - first child thread Visit = 1
    C - second child thread Visit = 1

AAAAA - main thread counter = 3
  BBB - first child thread Visit = 2
    C - second child thread Visit = 2

AAAAA - main thread counter = 2
  BBB - first child thread Visit = 3
    C - second child thread Visit = 3

AAAAA - main thread counter = 1
  BBB - first child thread Visit = 4
    C - second child thread Visit = 4
Main thread finished.
```

Fig 15.7 Output of `NewThreadsSecondDemo.java`

In the program of Fig.15.6 we defined two separate child classes. These two classes did not do very much. Apart from their command line output, they are identical. Indeed, we can create as many instances of the same class as we wish.

A good real-world example of this occurs with, say, transactions at an automatic teller machine or ATM. At any one moment, very large numbers of transactions are being carried out simultaneously. Each transaction will perform the same programming tasks. Online large banking systems are much more complicated than what we have here, of course, but they operate in much the same way.

In the next example, we create three `ChildThreads`, identical save for their having different names.

```
public class MultipleChildThreads {
  public static void main(String[] args){
    ChildThread t1 = new ChildThread("One");
    ChildThread t2 = new ChildThread("Two");
    ChildThread t3 = new ChildThread("Three");
    int counter = 5;
    while (counter > 0){
      try{
        System.out.println(" Back to the main thread " +
                          Counter = " + counter);
        t1.run();
        t2.run();
```

```
      t3.run();
      Thread.sleep(1000);
    }
    catch(InterruptedException iE){
      System.out.println("Main thread interruption");
    }
    counter--;
  }
  System.out.println("  Finished");
  }
}
class ChildThread implements Runnable{
  String name;
  int i = 10;
  Thread t;
  public ChildThread(String threadName){
    name = threadName;
    t = new Thread();
    t.setName(name);
    System.out.println("  Starting..." + name);
    t.start();
  }
  public void run(){
    try{
      System.out.println("  Thread " + name
                     + " : value of i = " + i);
      i--;
      Thread.sleep(1000);
    }
    catch(InterruptedException iE){
      System.out.println("  Interruprion in " + name);
    }
    System.out.println("  Thread " + name + " exiting");
  }
}
```

Fig 15.8 Multiple Identical Child Thread's

We can distinguish the three child Thread's using the String parameter threadName as in the child Thread constructor. With a little ingenuity, we could create a large number of such child Thread's in an array and execute a multi-dimensional threaded program for very little extra programming effort.

Java Quick and Easy

```
Starting...One
Starting...Two
Starting...Three
Back to the main thread. Counter = 5
Thread One : value of i = 10
Thread One exiting
Thread Two : value of i = 10
Thread Two exiting
Thread Three : value of i = 10
Thread Three exiting
Back to the main thread. Counter = 4
Thread One : value of i = 9
Thread One exiting
Thread Two : value of i = 9
Thread Two exiting
Thread Three : value of i = 9
Thread Three exiting
Back to the main thread. Counter = 3
Thread One : value of i = 8
Thread One exiting
Thread Two : value of i = 8
Thread Two exiting
Thread Three : value of i = 8
Thread Three exiting
Back to the main thread. Counter = 2
Thread One : value of i = 7
Thread One exiting
Thread Two : value of i = 7
Thread Two exiting
Thread Three : value of i = 7
Thread Three exiting
Back to the main thread. Counter = 1
Thread One : value of i = 6
Thread One exiting
Thread Two : value of i = 6
Thread Two exiting
Thread Three : value of i = 6
Thread Three exiting

Finished
```

Fig 15.9 Output of `MultipleChildThreads.java`

179

Thread Priorities

Not all Thread's are of equal importance. Some Thread's may need to be actioned infrequently while others need to be called more often. This occurs, for example, when data is being transferred to or from a hard disk in blocks. The actual data buffering may be the activity which consumes most of the time. But this will be suspended once the buffer is full and the data is written somewhere before the buffer is flushed. The main Thread will transfer the data to the buffer and set up a counter. Once the counter value is reached, the main Thread goes to sleep while the child Thread, which transfers the data and flushes the buffer, wakes up, does its work and then goes back to sleep.

The following example shows how two child Thread"s are assigned different priorities on a scale of 1 to 10. Obviously, the parent Thread is assigned the highest priority. The Thread class also defines three self-explanatory int constants, MAX_PRIORITY, MIN_PRIORITY and NORM_PRIORITY equal to 10, 1 and 5 respectively.

In the following example, the two child Thread's are visited in turn according to their priorities and total counts of the number of times they are active is reported at the end while the main Thread sleeps for 10 seconds. The priorities of the child threads are set to NORM_PRIORITY+2 and NORM_PRIORITY-2 or 7 and 3.

```
public class NewThreadsPriorityDemo {
  public static void main(String[] args){
    Thread.currentThread().setPriority
                      (Thread.MAX_PRIORITY);
    NewChildThread tH = new
        NewChildThread(Thread.NORM_PRIORITY+2);
    NewChildThread tL = new
        NewChildThread(Thread.NORM_PRIORITY-2);
    tH.start();
    tL.start();
    try{
      Thread.sleep(10000);
    }
    catch(InterruptedException iE){
      System.out.println("Sleep interrupted");
```

```
      }
      tH.stop();
      tL.stop();
      System.out.println
      ("  Visits to lower priority thread = " + tL.visit);
      System.out.println
      ("  Visits to higher priority thread = " + tH.visit);
    }
}
class NewChildThread implements Runnable{
  Thread t;
  long visit = 0;
  private volatile boolean running = true;
  public NewChildThread(int p){
    t = new Thread(this);
        // the Runnable thread is instantiating itself
    t.setPriority(p);
  }
  public void run(){
    while (running){
      visit++;
    }
  }
  public void stop(){
    running = false;
  }
  public void start(){
    t.start();
  }
}
```

Fig 15.10 Assigning Priorities to Thread*"s*

Notice the use of the modifier "volatile" in NewChildThread.java. If a varaiable is set as volatile, it means that it will not be optimized by the Java compiler and given a fixed value. It begins as true but changes each time the Thread"s change their states from running to sleeping.

Fig 15.11 below shows the output of the program NewThreadsPriorityDemo.java. The lower priority thread has been inside the processor 3,435,980,558 times as against the higher priority thread which made 4,012,091,992 visits to the processor. The

differences are not great, as the example shows. Setting of priority
levels and sleep times is not an exact science. Many factors – processor
speed, how the operating system works, the application"s resource
demands – all affect the overall performance..

```
Visits to lower priority thread = 3435980558
Visits to higher priority thread = 4012091992
```

Fig 15.11 Priority Counts for Multiple Threads

Threads with Graphics.

This next example shows how two `Thread`"s work together in a
graphical program. The left half of the screen displays alphabetic
letters, while the right displays colored circles of random size, color
and position. The `main`, parent `Thread`, does nothing except run the
two child `Thread`'s.

```java
import java.awt.*;
public class GraphicThreadExample extends Frame{
  Font f;
  int counter = 0;
  int size; xLeft = 20; yLeft = 100;
  int xRight = 520; yRight = 60;
  String s = "";
  Color c;
  public GraphicThreadExample(){
    f = new Font("Serif", Font.BOLD, 48);
    setSize(1000,1000);
    setLayout(null);
    setTitle("Graphics thread");
    setVisible(true);
    addWindowListener(new MyWindowAdapter());
  }
  public void paint(Graphics g){
    int len,rows,spare;
    String sub1,sub2;
    g.setFont(f);
    g.setColor(Color.blue);
    g.fillRect(0,0,500,1000);
    g.setColor(Color.yellow);
```

```
      g.fillRect(500,0,500,1000);
      len = s.length();
      rows = len/20;
      spare = len%20;
      for ( int i = 0; i < rows; i++){
        sub1 = s.substring(20*i,20*i+19);
        g.drawString(sub1,xLeft,yLeft + i*50);
      }
      sub2 = s.substring(rows*20);
      g.drawString(sub2,xLeft,yLeft + rows*50);
      g.setColor(c);
      g.fillOval(xRight,yRight,size,size);
  }
  public void runThreads(){
    LeftThread lT = new LeftThread("Left");
    RightThread rT = new RightThread("Right");
    while (counter < 100){
      try{
        lT.run();
        rT.run();
        Thread.sleep(1000);
      }
      catch(InterruptedException iE){
        System.out.println("Interrupted Exception...");
      }
      counter++;
    }
  }
  private class LeftThread implements Runnable{
    Thread t;
    String name;
    public LeftThread(String threadName){
      name = threadName;
      t = new Thread();
      t.setName(name);
      t.start();
    }
    public void run(){
      try{
        s = s + (char) (counter%26 + 65) + " ";
        repaint();
        Thread.sleep(1000);
      }
      catch(InterruptedException iE){
        System.out.println("Exception...");
      }
```

```java
    }
}
  private class RightThread implements Runnable{
    Thread t;
    String name;
    public RightThread(String threadName){
      name = threadName;
      t = new Thread();
      t.setName(name);
      t.start();
    }
    public void run(){
      int r;
      try{
        r = (int) Math.round(Math.random()*10);
        switch(r){
            case 0:c = Color.red; break;
            case 1:c = Color.green; break;
            case 2:c = Color.blue; break;
            case 3:c = Color.pink; break;
            case 4:c = Color.orange; break;
            case 5:c = Color.black; break;
            case 6:c = Color.white; break;
            case 7:c = Color.darkGray; break;
            case 8:c = Color.lightGray; break;
            case 9:c = Color.magenta;
          }
        xRight = 500+(int)Math.round(Math.random()*400);
        yRight = 50+(int) Math.round(Math.random()*900);
        size = 20 + (int) Math.round(Math.random()*40);
        repaint();
        Thread.sleep(1000);
      }
      catch(InterruptedException iE){
        System.out.println("Exception...");
      }
    }
  }
}
public static void main(String args[]){
  GraphicThreadExample gT =new GraphicThreadExample();
  gT.runThreads();
}
}
```

Fig 15.12 Threads and Graphics

Fig 15.13 Threads and Graphics

Chapter 15 Exercises

1. Write a program with a single colored disk in the centre of a `Frame` of size 300 x 300. The foreground disk is in the main `Thread` and the background color is in a child `Thread`. Each `Thread` is awake for 500 milliseconds. As a `Thread` wakes up, it becomes a different random color.

2. Develop the program in Question 1 above to show three colored disks side by side in three child `Thread"`s.

3. Write a program with two `Threads`. `Thread` 1 increments a long value starting from zero. `Thread` 2 counts from 0 to 65535. `Thread` 1 sleeps for 100 milliseconds and wakes up to begin counting while `Thread` 2 sleeps for 100 milliseconds. When `Thread` 2 wakes up, the value which `Thread` 1 has reached is output and its count starts again at zero. When `Thread` 1 wakes up, the UNICODE character in `Thread` 2 is displayed and `Thread` 2 goes back to sleep. The whole cycle repeats for 100 times.

4. Create a multithreaded program which divides the screen into four equal different colored squares and writes "1", "2", "3", "4" in the center

of each of the squares, as the Thread's cycle. The numbers are removed in turn, so that only one number is shown at any one time.

5. Write a Thread'ed program which will move a colored ball across the screen from left to right. Previously we did this using a simple counter time delay while we changed the ball"s position (See Fig 11.2). Instead, change the ball"s position using a Thread and a sleep command.

6. Add a second ball to the program in Question 5. It moves from right to left, at a different screen y–value, is of a different color, and a different size. One ball sleeps for longer than the other so they seem to be moving at different speeds.

7. Write a program with two Thread's. Each Thread controls a different TextField labelled "Left" and "Right". Both display a number count starting from 0,1,2... etc. A mouse click stops the current count and starts the other from its last value.

8. Write a threaded program which divides a Frame into two halves. The left half lists all the numbers of the Fibonacci sequence 0,1,1,2... where every number is the sum of the two previous numbers. The right hand half of the screen calculates the square roots of the natural numbers. Each Thread is awake for a period of time which you can vary to make the program run smoothly.

9. Modify the program in Question 7 above to add priorities to the two Thread"s. Make one Thread MAX_PRIORITY and the other MIN_PRIORITY. Output the number of times each Thread has been awake.

10. Modify the program from Question 6 to show any number of colored balls of varying sizes and colors moving independently at different speeds.

Java Quick and Easy

Chapter 16   Java on a Network

Java has a number of useful libraries to provide functionality to network programmers and designers. The package `java.net` contains methods for all the low-level operations of connections between networked objects. The first example shows how to connect to the Internet via a Uniform Resource Locator or URL.

```
import java.net.*;
import java.io.*;
import java.util.Date;
class URLDemo{
  public static void main(String[] args)
                  throws MalformedURLException{
    int c;
    URL hp = new
        URL("http://cpayne.com:80/Downloads/index.html");
    System.out.println();
    System.out.println(" Protocol : "
                              + hp.getProtocol());
    System.out.println(" Port : " + hp.getPort());
    System.out.println(" Host : " + hp.getHost());
    System.out.println(" File : " + hp.getFile());
    System.out.println(" Ext : " + hp.toExternalForm());
    System.out.println();
  }
}
```

Fig 16.1 The Parts of a URL

```
Protocol : http
Port : 80
Host : cpayne.com
File : /Downloads/index.html
Ext : http://cpayne.com:80/Downloads/index.html
```

Fig 16.2 Output of `URLDemo.java`

The program `URLDemo.java` shows the parts of a URL including the protocol, **http,** the port number, 80, and the file entry to the directory,

187

which is, by convention, unless you specify otherwise, called *index.html*.

We can also make a full Internet connection using the method `URLConnection`. This enables us to read the text content of remote web pages as in the following example.

```java
import java.net.*;
import java.io.*;
import java.util.Date;

class UCDemo{
  public static void main(String[] args) throws Exception{
    int c;
    URL urlHP = new URL("http://cpayne.com/BG60/");
    URLConnection urlHPCon = urlHP.openConnection();
    System.out.println();
    System.out.println("  Date : " +
                        new Date(urlHPCon.getDate()));
    System.out.println("  Content-Type : " +
                        urlHPCon.getContentType());
    System.out.println("  Expires : " +
                        urlHPCon.getExpiration());
    System.out.println("  Last Modified : " +
                new Date(urlHPCon.getLastModified()));
    int len = urlHPCon.getContentLength();
    if (len > 0){
      InputStream input = urlHPCon.getInputStream();
      int i = len;
      while (
         (( c = input.read()) != -1) && ( --i > 0)){
            System.out.print((char) c);
      }
      input.close();
    }
    else
    {
      System.out.println("No content available.");
    }
  }
}
```

Fig 16.3 Returning the Contents of a Remote Web Page

```
Date : Fri Jun 12 14:18:08 SGT 2015
Content-Type : text/html
Expires : 0
Last Modified : Mon May 18 15:33:33 SGT 2015
<html>
<head>
</head>
<body>
<p>Click <a href = "http://cpayne.com/BG60/BG60.zip">here</a> to download file B
G60.zip (size = 179MB) containing the birthday photographs</p>
</body>
</html>
```

Fig 16.4 Output of UCDemo.java

Internet addresses are usually 4 bytes in length (There is a 6-byte type which is not yet common.). Obviously *cpayne.com* is easier to remember than 195.26.89.15 but the numeric form is needed to route the message through the Internet from sender to receiver. The translation of the familiar URL to its numeric form is the job of the Domain Name Service (DNS), a complicated hierarchical online service which allows any valid Internet name to be converted to its Internet Protocol (IP) address.

The following program shows how Java will behave like a simple DNS and return the 4-byte address for our own machine - the *localhost* - and two other personal web URL"s. Note three different methods for accessing the address.

```
import java.net.*;
class InternetAddresses {
  public static void main(String[] args)
            throws UnknownHostException{
    InetAddress address = InetAddress.getLocalHost();
    System.out.println("  " + address);
    address = InetAddress.getByName("cpayne.com");
    System.out.println("  " + address);
    InetAddress SW[] =
       InetAddress.getAllByName("www.lipapublishing.com");
    for ( int i = 0; i < SW.length; i++) {
      System.out.println("  " + SW[i]);
    }
  }
}
```

Fig 16.5 Returning 4-byte Internet Addresses

189

```
Chris-PC/192.168.100.5
cpayne.com/195.26.89.15
www.lipapublishing.com/195.26.90.15
```

Fig 16.6 Output of `InternetAddresses.java`

Sockets

A socket is a virtual specific connection on a network, like a telephone number. If I make a phone call to you, I must know your number. If we are to converse, then the two numbers, yours and mine, must be linked together for the duration of the call. Sockets work in the same way. There must be a sending, or server socket, and a receiving, or client, socket. A socket and a port are not the same thing. A socket is the combination of an IP address and a port number. Port numbers are two bytes long, which gives up to 65536 different ports per IP address. This allows for multiple connections to the same IP or URL.

The port numbers 0-1023 are the "Well Known Ports" which are used for particular special applications. For example, a web server on using the Hypertext Transaction Protocol or **http,** will always use port 80. The File Transfer Protocol **(ftp)** always passes through port 19 and port 25 is dedicated to email. (Although these days, most email traffic is web-based and uses port 80 like other web applications.) The port numbers which are not allocated, 1024 – 65535 are available for client use.

Why then, if the Internet uses so few standard port values, should we need over 65,000 possible numbers? The reason is that many organizations need to have multiple users accessed via the same IP address. For example, a large hotel may offer free Internet connectivity to its guests, all of whom might be connected simultaneously via the same Internet connection. When a hotel guest connects to the hotel server, the server allocates a random port address to the machine which the guest is using.

Java Quick and Easy

If the guest now wants to visit some web site, the ISP binds the IP address of the server hosting the page and creates a five-part "association" made up of the protocol e.g. TCP, plus the the IP address and the port numbers of the two machines, the guest"s and the remote web server"s sockets.

Here is a simple example using a Java class called `SocketClient`. It will not do anything on its own without a server socket anymore than a telephone will ring without both sender and receiver having valid phone numbers. So we will also later need a `SocketServer` class to complete the connection.

There is another simplification we use while we are getting up to speed. In these first examples, we are putting both the client and the server on the same machine, the so-called *localhost*. In the real world, there would be some physical link between two different machines such as a USB (Universal Serial Bus) cable, Ethernet or some other connection, maybe Wi-Fi, between the client and the server. But, until we get the programs up and running, we will get them working properly on a single machine.

What the following program does is to define a client socket by its Internet address and port number. The package `java.net` provides the class method for doing this. Then, once the connection is made, it can be written to via an `OutputStreamWriter` instance with a call to the server. Conversation must be two-way, so we also have a `InputStreamReader` to receive character input from the Server. The program is shown in Fig 16.7.

```
import java.net.*;
import java.io.*;
public class SocketClient{
  public static void main(String[] args){
    String host = "localhost";
    int port = 2000;
    StringBuffer instr = new StringBuffer();
    String timeStamp;
    try{
      InetAddress address =
```

```
            InetAddress.getByName(host);
      Socket connection = new Socket(address, port);
      BufferedOutputStream bos = new
      BufferedOutputStream(connection.getOutputStream());
      OutputStreamWriter osw =
                   new OutputStreamWriter(bos);
      timeStamp = new java.util.Date().toString();
      String process =
               "Calling the socket server on "
               + host + " port " + port + " at "
               + timeStamp + (char)13 ;
      osw.write(process);
      osw.flush();
      BufferedInputStream bis = new
      BufferedInputStream(connection.getInputStream());
      InputStreamReader isr =
               new InputStreamReader(bis);
      int c;
      while (( c = isr.read()) != 13){
        instr.append((char) c);
      }
      connection.close();
      System.out.println(isr);
   }
  catch(IOException ioE){
     System.out.println();
     System.out.println("    IOException..." + ioE);
     System.out.println();
  }
  catch(Exception e){
     System.out.println("    Excepotion e..."+ e);
  }
 }
}
```

Fig 16.7 Setting up a Client Socket for Writing and Reading

```
IOException...java.net.ConnectException: Connection refused: connect
```

Fig 16.8 Output of `SocketClient.java`.

This terse little message appears whenever there is no connection. The reason for that is that we do not yet have a server to respond. It is possible to create a server program which will respond to a single client. But to be general, it is better if our server can be made more versatile by giving it the ability to handle multiple clients. The following program does just that by using multiple threads. It uses an infinite `while` loop in the `main()` method as it waits for clients to talk to it. Then it returns an acknowledgement. For each client request, a new thread is created and processed.

```java
import java.net.*;
import java.io.*;
import java.util.*;
public class SocketServer implements Runnable{
  private Socket s;
  private String timeDate;
  private int iD;
  SocketServer(Socket s,int i){
    this.s = s;
    this.iD = i;
  }
  public static void main(String[] args){
    int port = 2000;
    int count = 0;
    try{
      ServerSocket socket1 = new ServerSocket(port);
      System.out.println("SocketServer initialized");
      while (true){
        Socket s = socket1.accept();
        Runnable serverConnection =
                        new SocketServer(s,count++);
        Thread serverThread =
                        new Thread(serverConnection);
        serverThread.start();
      }
    }
    catch(Exception e){}
  }

  public void run(){
    try{
      BufferedInputStream iS =
      new BufferedInputStream(s.getInputStream());
      InputStreamReader iSR = new
                        InputStreamReader(iS);
```

```
    int i;
    StringBuffer sB = new StringBuffer();
    while ((i = iSR.read()) != 13) {
      sB.append((char) i);
    }
    System.out.println(sB);
    timeDate = new java.util.Date().toString();
    String returnString =
    "SocketServer responded at " +
                        timeDate + (char)13;
    BufferedOutputStream oS =
      new BufferedOutputStream(s.getOutputStream());
    OutputStreamWriter oSW =
            new OutputStreamWriter(oS,"ASCII");
    oSW.write(returnString);
    oSW.flush();
  }
  catch(Exception e){}
  try{
    s.close();
  }
  catch(IOException e){}
  }
}
```

Fig 16.9 Server Side Socket Processing

Fig 16.10 is the output of the client–side request. Fig 16.11 is the response from the program shown in Fig 16.9. Basic communication has been established.

```
SocketServer responded at Fri Jun 12 16:29:52 SGT 2015
```

Fig 16.10 Output of Fig 16.9 – the Client Side

```
SocketServer initialized
Calling socket server on localhost port 2000 at Fri Jun 12 16:29:52 SGT 2015
```

Fig 16.11 The Client-Server Output Screens – the Server Side

Java Quick and Easy

Datagrams

Internet data is passed in packets of data called *datagrams*. In addition to the data payload, datagram packets will need to include a substantial additional metadata including sender and destination addresses, coding formats, encryption keys, timing bytes and a good deal more. Since they will often be sent a long way and need to pass through numerous routing stations, long packets may be broken up – fragmented. So one of the fields in the datagram contains the fragmentation sequence details. (The basic structure of a datagram is shown in Fig 16.12.)

Java provides a `DatagramPacket` class for manipulation of datagram input/output in the package java.net.*; There are four constructors for `DatagramPacket`:

```
DatagramPacket(byte data[], int size);
DatagramPacket(byte data[], int offset,int size);
DatagramPacket(byte data[], int size,
                  InetAddress ipAddres, int port);
DatagramPacket(byte data[], int offset,
            int size, InetAddress ipAddress,int port);
```

The main methods of `DatagramPacket` are

```
InetAddress getAddress()
```
returns destination Internet address.
```
int getPort
```
returns port number of the destination
```
byte[] getData
```
returns the raw data of the packet
```
int getLength()
```
returns the length of raw data

Each `DatagramPacket` object can communicate with a `DatagramSocket` for sending and receiving data as shown in the next program example. It is a simple program which defines a datagram client–server system inside the *localhost* machine.

The Transaction Control Protocol/Internet Protocol or TCP/IP defines a complicated structure for datagrams. In addition to the raw data transmitted between source and destination, metatdata for addressing, data checking, fragmenting etc. is added to the front of the data payload according to the following arrangement.

Frame Header	IP Header	TCP Header	Data Payload	Frame Trailer

Fig 16.12 A Transmitted Datagram Packet

In this model, the IP 4-byte addresses are contained in the IP Header. The port numbers are fields inside the TCP Header. The Frame Header and Trailer (or Footer) carry information about the physical structure of the packet of data, including a timing preamble and the physical addresses of the network devices.

Here is a very simple java program which uses datagrams. Both the client and the server reside on the *localhost* at ports 20000 and 20001.

```java
import java.net.*;
public class Datagrams {
  public static int serverPort = 20000;
  public static int clientPort = 20001;
  public static int bufferSize = 1024;
                // Can be any reasonable size.
                // This is a mid-range number
  public static DatagramSocket dS;
  public static byte buffer[] = new byte[bufferSize];

  public static void Server() throws Exception{
    int pos = 0;
    System.out.println("This is the Server");
    while (true){
      int c = System.in.read();
      switch(c){
        case -1 : System.out.println
                        ("Server quits!");//CTRL+"C"
                return;
        case '\r': break;                   // CR
        case '\n': dS.send
                  (new DatagramPacket(buffer,pos,
```

```
                InetAddress.getLocalHost(),clientPort));
                pos = 0;
                break;                            // CRLF
        default  : buffer[pos++] = (byte) c;
      } //switch
    }     // while
  }
  public static void Client() throws Exception{
    System.out.println("This is the Client");
    while (true){
      DatagramPacket p =
            new DatagramPacket(buffer, buffer.length);
      dS.receive(p);
      System.out.println(new String(p.getData(),
                                  0, p.getLength()));
    }
  }
  public static void main(String[] args)
                        throws Exception{
    if (args.length == 1) {
      dS = new DatagramSocket(serverPort);
      Server();
    }
    else
    {
      dS = new DatagramSocket(clientPort);
      Client();
    }
  }
}
```

Fig 16.13 Sending and Receiving Datagram Packets

As in the previous example, to run this program we need to compile it and set up two command line windows, one for the server and one for the client. In the server window, type

```
>java Datagrams c
```

where c is any single character. to start the server.

In the client window, type

```
>java Datagrams
```

The program will then allow you to send messages from server to client between the two windows.

```
This is the Server
Hello client!!
```

Fig 16.14 Sending and Receiving Datagrams - The Server Side

```
This is the Client
Hello client!!
```

Fig 16.15 Output of `Datagrams.java` *– The Client side*

Chapter 16 Exercises

1. Add a webpage to a remote website and write a Java program to return a listing of the page"s HTML.

2. Write a Java applet which will return the IP address of a webpage URL entered in a `JTextField`. It returns the details as `JLabels`.

3. Modify the applet in Question 2 to return the full URL address of the webpage.

4. Write a Java `applet` which will enter a web URL in a `JTextField` and return the 4–byte IP address of the entered address.

5. Write a Java program to enter the URL address of a *.TXT* file and to download the contents of the file.

6. Write a Java program which will send and receive messages between a server and a client. The server sends " I am the server" and the the client replies with " And I am the client".

7. Write a Java JApplet which will read a datagram and return a JLabel with the size of the datagram.

8. Modify the program in Fig 16.13 to a Windows interface using the Abstract Windows Toolkit. The server and client sides are two halves of the same screen.

9. Develop your program from Question 8 to add a test for the ESC key. When the ESC is pressed on the server side, the user gets a message inviting them to send the message by answering "Y" or "N".

10. Develop the program from Question 9 to reject, with the JLabel "Message too short!", any message which is shorter than 6 characters long.

Java Quick and Easy

Appendix A   What is Object-Orientation?

These days, computer programs can be millions of lines long and used in life-critical applications. Indeed, we have, as a society, put much of our social organization in the electronic hands of computer programs. Programs of that size will be prone to errors of logic and the larger a piece of code is, the more errors it is going to have. One solution to the problem of growing program size would be to test the program exhaustively. Unfortunately, testing is expensive and takes time and there is no guarantee either that the testing regime will find all the possible errors. There may be some nasty surprises down the line.

A better solution is to build large programs from small units of code which have been thoroughly tested and reusable. This is standard engineering practice in areas such as house building or automobiles. A house builder can rely on the units he uses such as bricks or planks or windows. All he does is to assemble the finished house from these elementary components.

So it is with object-oriented programming. Programs are built from "objects", pre-existing reusable program fragments which can be bolted together to make bigger original programs. These objects are defined by a 'class', the template which allows for multiple instances of the object, as required. Object classes are collected into libraries which are, themselves, bundled into 'packages'. To create a new program, a programmer will use these ready-made objects which can communicate between each other by messages e.g. the click of a button object inside a window object. When the program is run, the programmer can arrange that a message is sent from the button object to the window object to change, maybe, its background color.

The program code of both these objects and the messages they send have been thoroughly tested so that the user can be sure they will work properly and safely every time. The programmer has no access to the underlying code of any of these library objects so he cannot introduce new errors of his own.

Each class contains data and methods, functions which manipulate the data. Program code from outside the class can only access the data and methods of a class via its standard interfaces i.e. the predetermined message-sending mechanism. The message might be, e.g. a string of data or some numeric value. This ring fence around a class is called **encapsulation**. It ensures that external events cannot corrupt the data and methods inside the class. New classes are created by a programmer and the same rules of encapsulation apply to these new programs also.

```
.
class FileMaintenance{
  public FileMaintenance(){
    InitializeFile i = new InitializeFile();
    UpdateFile u = new UpdateFile();
    ReportResults r = new ReportResults();
  }
  public static void main(String args){
    FileMaintenance fM = new FileMaintenance();
  }
}
class InitializeFile{}
class UpdateFile{}
class ReportResults{}
```

Fig A.1 Abstraction – The First Stage of a Program to be Developed by Step-Wise Refinement

A very useful feature of Java is **abstraction** which allows for systematic program design using datanames for Java classes, methods and data variables which are also self-documenting i.e they can be identified by self-descriptive names. Abstraction allows us to write software using simple instructions which may refer to classes whose body of methods still has to be written.

The program in Fig A.1 does nothing at all, save define the upper level of a program for file maintenance. The point of abstraction is that the programmer can develop this application top-down by expanding the four classes in a step-wise way while deferring the writing of the nitty-gritty details as long as possible. This way of developing software allows the programmer to add gradual refinements as the code gets written and new classes are added to the design.

It is also a good way of testing the code. As the program expands, the code gets recompiled and retested over and over again. If problems arise during this cycle of step-wise refinement, one can quickly locate the problem object.

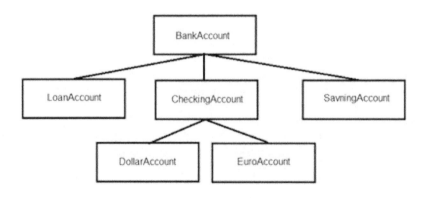

Fig A.2 Inheritance of the `BankAccount.java` *class*

Most object-oriented programs make use of **inheritance.** Classes, both library-derived and programmer-written may be arranged in a hierarchy. For example, suppose we have a class called "`BankAccount.java`". It will have a range of methods to do such things as open and close the account, report the balance, print a statement etc.

Bank accounts exist in several different forms - checking account, savings account, credit card account and so on. All the accounts will have common methods inherited from the parent class. But all will also have methods local only to themselves.

When defining the methods of the child account classes, only those methods specific to the child account need be rewritten, otherwise a class can use the methods which it inherits from its superclass.

Suppose though, that the class `DollarAccount` wanted to use a different method for opening an account than the one it inherits from its parent. It can do so by writing a new version of a method "`OpenAccount`" local to `DollarAccount`. This is called "**overriding**". The class "`DollarAccount`" could, though, still use the parent version of "`OpenAccount`". In Java, this is done via the prefix "`super.`" before the parent method name.

Polymorphism is the name given to the process by which the same class can be used to handle different input configurations. In the above example of a bank account we might have a single method for depositing money to an account. The method will appear the same to the programmer regardless of denomination of the currency – dollars or euros. The program will include multiple constructors so that a single class and its methods can be used for different currencies without the programmer needing to write multiple separate classes to handle each currency separately..

Java collects related classes into 'packages' . These packages can be imported into `applet`'s and applications and their individual class files can be used by the importing programs. Each class will contain variables and constant values which may be primitive types or other classes and methods which are small programs to perform certain tasks. Class definitions are only templates for objects which can be incorporated into larger programs. The process of creating an object from its class definition is called 'instantiation' and occurs when the class constructor is executed. One class definition can give rise to an infinite number of objects.

The objects of the package can be incorporated into new classes from which new objects can be created. Since the original packages are completely reliable, the correctness or otherwise of the final application is down only to how the programmer assembles the pre-defined objects.

Modern Java applications may run to thousands of imported packages and classes, but there can usually only ever be one `main()` method which starts the whole application.

Java has reduced the amount of time which used to be spent on program testing, because of its encapsulated reliable classes and packages. Testing of completed applications is still important but testing times are much reduced because the building blocks of the programs, the Java classes, are guaranteed to be safe and reliable. Faster development has another benefit. It means that much larger applications can be built to higher standards of reliability.

The essence of good software is that it is safe. Because of security concerns, java has lost its importance as a language for Internet development but its versatility and its exception handling capabilities mean that it has found many new application areas in the development of critical applications where safety is of paramount concern.

We usually want our programs to be interactive and to work in real time. Nowadays with multi-core multi-processing and low cost memory plus offline storage, real-time interactivity is the new norm. Java assists the developer of interactive programs by some useful functionality.

A feature of the Java compiler is that it optimizes the byte code output for maximum efficiency. As the JVM executes the program, unused data and program code is discarded and overwritten. If a window object is closed, for example, to be returned to later, then it is more efficient for the computer to destroy the memory image of the window and recreate it from scratch on recall. This is because processor operations are so much faster than memory access operations. This process is known as 'garbage collection' – the continuous tidying up of the executable program to minimize its size and to speed up overall performance.

Java does have its drawbacks and these have attracted ongoing criticism of the language ever since its birth. Amongst these is tha fact that it is essentially an interpreted language. When a Java `.class` file of byte codes is executed, it must be translated to native machine code in real time. This is a relatively slow process compared with running a compiled executable object file.

Another feature of byte code is that it is fairly easy to reverse engineer to the original source, which compromises the security of the copyright of a program idea.

Both of these features can be partially overcome by resort to third-party software which can translate the byte codes to the appropriate machine code. The author has no experience of these but common opinion has it that they are not always one hundred percent effective in speeding up compiled Java code or of preventing reverse engineering of software to recover the original source code.

In spite of these two problems though, Java sums up over sixty years of program language development and includes most of the desirable features of program design learnt over that time. Large programs can be produced relatively quickly and safely with good programmer productivity. More important, Java's notation and lexis means that subsequent maintenance is also done efficiently, since maintenance is a major part of the programmer's work.

Appendix B   Jerry"s Auto Shop

This is a long student exercise which may be set to students studying Java for the first time, It should take about 6 hours to complete and students should be able to tackle it after they have completed Chapters 1– 10.

The Specification

Jerry runs an auto repair shop called "Jerry"s Auto Shop". He accepts customers in 3–hour slots, working from 6 00 am until 6 00 pm. His first slot is from 6 00 am until 9 00 am and last slot is 3 00 pm – 6 00 pm. Your job is to create a form and data-entry method, written in Java, to be used for making online advance bookings. The form will consist of a user-friendly interface with the following fields.

Field Label	Type of Object
Customer name	`TextField`
Customer phone number	`TextField`
Customer email	`TextField`
Date of appointment	`Choice` lists (MM–DD–YY)
Slot available	`Choice` list
Method of payment (Check, Credit card, Cash, Account)	`CheckboxGroup`
Details of problem	`TextArea`

The top of the form has a heading – a label in a suitable font and color. Jerry"s logo is in the top right-hand corner of the screen. The logo is in a file, "*Jerrys_Auto_Shop_Logo.jpg*" which you need to create separately with a graphics editor.

In the bottom right hand corner of the window are two buttons, marked "Save" and "Cancel". Pressing "Save" will cause all the current data to be saved to a file called "*Jerrys_Auto_Shop.dat*" After "Save" has been pressed and the data saved, the screen is reset to its opening position with no data visible. Also, a message "Data saved" appears at the bottom left hand corner of the screen. This message disappears when the next entry is made. Pressing "Cancel" causes the screen to go back to its start condition and the message shown is "Booking cancelled".

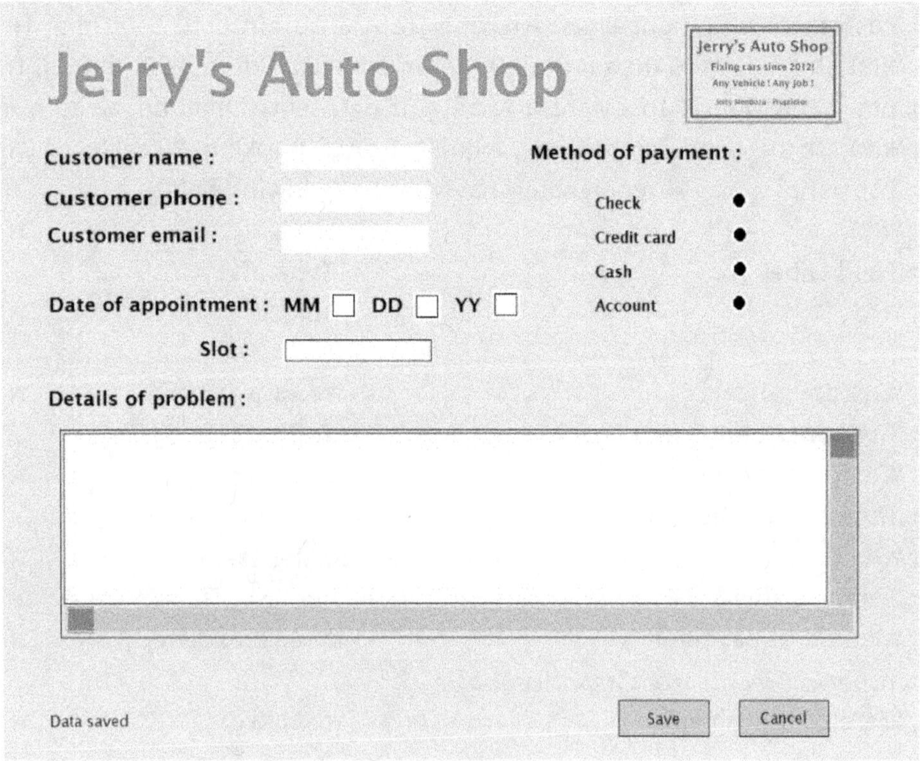

Fig B.1 The GUI for Jerry"s Auto Shop

Java Quick and Easy

Appendix C   Further Reading and Useful Websites

Java has a wide literature, much of which is duplicated. One needs a good reference book since memorizing the thousands of classes and methods in Java is not something one wants, or needs, to do.

The books I like best are :

Java 2 The Complete Reference by Patrick Naughton and Herbert Schildt. Third Edition dated 1999. Published McGraw Hill. This is also available as an e-Book. The edition is now fifteen years old but I find no need to replace it with anything newer.

Computing Concepts with Java 2 Essentials by Cay Horstmann
Second Edition dated 2000 Published by John Wiley & Sons Ltd.,

Websites

ORACLE, the owners of Java, have a large website for assistance to java users and developers. The complete list of packages and classes published by ORACLE can be found at:

http://docs.oracle.com/javase/7/docs/api/

There is a great deal of free Java tutorial websites. The most important is the ORACLE site at

http://docs.oracle.com/javase/tutorial/

Other sites, of varying accessibility include. This list is not exhaustive by a long way – most colleges which offer online education provide basic courses in Java.

http://www.tutorialspoint.com/java
https://www.udemy.com/java-tutorial

http://www.learnjavaonline.org/
http://www.lynda.com/Java-training-tutorials/1077-0.html
http://www.eclipsetutorial.sourceforge.net/
http://www.freejavaguide.com/corejava.htm
http://www.javacodegeeks.com

Java is also the subject of a large number of blogs. These sites can be useful when researching solutions to Java programming problems which are not covered in the basic texts.

http://stackoverflow.com/
http://www.programcreek.com/2012/11/
                    top-100-java-developers-blogs
http://www.javacodegeeks.com
http://www.topjavablogs.com
http://www.java.net/blogfront
http://www.baeldung.com/java-blogs

Appendix D Supporting Materials

Supporting material for teachers is available online

Included is

1. Source code listings of the programs in the book;
2. Microsoft PowerPoint slides for a course of 16 lectures based on the chapters of the book
3. Class exercises for each of the lectures ready to print in Microsoft Word .DOCX format;
4. The source code for the solution of the application JerrysAutoShop.java from Appendix B
5. Selected solutions of laboratory exercises.
6. Additional Chapter 17 – Java for Android Tablets

Purchasers of the hard copy version of *Java Quick and Easy* may download this material by visiting :

http://lipapublishing.com/Downloads/

Download code 13OAFC31

Index

ISBN 978-971-9678-03-8